THE
UPSIDE
OF
DOWN

ALSO BY CHARLES KENNY

Getting Better

THE
UPSIDE
OF
DOWN

Why the Rise of the Rest
Is Good for the West

Charles Kenny

BASIC BOOKS
NEW YORK

Books published by Basic Books are available at special
discounts for bulk purchases in the United States by
corporations, institutions, and other organizations. For more
information, please contact the Special Markets Department
at the Perseus Books Group, 2300 Chestnut Street, Suite 200,
Philadelphia, PA 19103, or call (800) 810-4145, ext. 5000, or
e-mail special.markets@perseusbooks.com.

Book design by Linda Mark

A CIP catalog record for this book is available from the
Library of Congress.
ISBN: 978-0-465-06473-1

10 9 8 7 6 5 4 3 2 1

To Charlotte, Alexandra, Marguerite, Isla, and Julia

Contents

Preface

I MAGINE YOU WERE ABOUT TO BE BORN. And somehow, you got the choice as to *where* you'd be born. Would you choose Asia, or Africa, or Europe, or the Americas? If you had any sense, you'd be likely to choose one of the countries of North America or Europe—or another safely developed country, like Australia, New Zealand, Japan, or Singapore—not least because your chance of surviving the first years of life would be higher there than anywhere else. When you reached an age to appreciate such things, you'd probably also be richer, better educated, safer, and more secure in your rights. You'd be more likely to have an interesting job and a long and enjoyable retirement. All in all, by whatever measure, your quality of life would almost certainly be higher.

Of course, you might draw the short straw—poverty in the West can be soul-crushing and life-shortening just as wealth in India or Africa can afford all the luxuries the world has to offer. But on average, the advantages of being born in the West are clear.

Now imagine that the choice you are given is not *where* to be born, but *when*—anytime between the dawn of *Homo sapiens* and today. Again, your choice would be clear—in fact, it would be even more specific. Today is the time to be born, whether your priority is a long, healthy life, or opportunities to learn, or options in what to do and consume, or freedom to live as you choose. Whether you will live in Africa or Asia or Europe or the Americas, no time has been as good a time to be alive as now.

There remain, again, millions of horrible exceptions—lives cut short by disease, poverty, violence, or neglect. But those exceptions are rarer today than ever.

Put those two choices together. Being born today in the West is like winning the birth lottery for the human species. And nothing that has happened over the last few years—the global recession, tensions between the United States and Iran or North Korea—has changed that.

There are fears, however, that the quality of life in the West has reached a peak. That China or India will soon overtake Europe and America, leaving them in decline. Or that global progress will be reversed by shortages—of oil, or copper, or water, or cooler air. This book addresses those fears. It suggests that the only thing better than being born today in America or Europe will be the chance to be born tomorrow in those very same places. And it suggests that the rise of "the Rest" is one big reason why that is true.

There is surely much to argue with in the pages that follow. I believe that my statements about the past—about things like the impact of trade and migration, or the mortality risk of terror, or the rate of progress in developing countries—are made on the basis of the best academic literature. Of course, that is a judgment call, and I do not always fully summarize the arguments on both sides. And when it comes to forecasts of the future, these are necessarily best guesses. Perhaps the developing world will sink back into the morass of low growth—and perhaps young people in the West will turn their backs on it.

But the reason predictions about the future of humans are necessarily imperfect is that we can change that future. And I hope that enlightened self-interest in the West about the benefits of the rising Rest is one of the forces that can help push the future in a positive direction.

I say all that writing as a Westerner. I am lucky enough to have been born to a European father and an American mother, to have been brought up in the United Kingdom, and to have lived my adult life in the United States. My family and my wife's family are made up of two generations of intercontinental marriages—five of them, all but one transatlantic. So when I write about what global changes mean for Europe and America, or what Europe and the United States should do about them, I am writing about "us" and about "our" response.

But I have been focused on (and sometimes lived in) Asian, Latin American, and African countries for most of my career. I'm a proud uncle of a niece born in China, daughter to my brother and sister-in-law, who met while working in Hong Kong. My father-in-law was born, raised, and worked in Argentina, and my wife spent her first years in that country. So while I think of myself as Western, I speak from considerable personal experience when I say there is much that the Rest can offer people in the United States and Europe. My closest family and I have benefited immeasurably from a world of closer connections and expanding opportunities—to explore, to make a living, to fall in love, to raise a family.

And I hope my children, nieces, and any future nephews will benefit even more. If the Rest gets wealthier, healthier, more educated, more democratic, and more peaceful, it will have even more to offer. So while the West will remain the best place to live in the world for most people for most of the foreseeable future, reaching out to the Rest will make our lives far richer, more interesting—and even happier.

CHAPTER ONE

Losing an Empire
and Finding a Role

A S AMERICA'S RECOVERY FROM the global recession that began in 2007–2008 staggers on, undocumented immigrants in the country are heading back home in search of a better life. Two US-led wars in the last decade have dragged toward an end charitably described as "mission not completely failed." That the country could avoid default a couple of years ago only by stopping pretty much all of the other business of government bar naming post offices for a few weeks is reminiscent of the last days of the Roman Republic. Meanwhile, across the Atlantic, the Euro Zone, so obviously an ill-matched patchwork, is held together by fraying threads. Ninety percent of the French population reckons their kids will be poorer than they are. What a grim time to be from the West.

In fact, argument already rages over whether the United States— the anchor player for Team West—is still even the largest world economy. Writing in his book *Eclipse: Living in the Shadow of China's Economic Dominance*, former International Monetary Fund (IMF) economist Arvind Subramanian suggests that China has already overtaken the United States as the largest economy in terms of purchasing power parity (which adjusts exchange rates to account for the different prices people pay for goods and services across countries). The World Bank's statistics suggest that the US economy is still larger, perhaps by as much as 45 percent. But even China pessimists agree that it is only a matter of a few years until the Middle Kingdom's 1.3 billion people produce more than do the 310 million living in America. Subramanian concludes that "the economic dominance of China relative to the United States is more imminent (it may have already begun), will be more broad-based and could be as large in magnitude in the next 20 years as that of the United Kingdom in the halcyon days of empire or the United States in the aftermath of World War II."[1]

And China is only one part (if a large part) of a global transformation in the fortunes of the world's developing countries. India, like China, more than doubled the size of its economy over the first decade of the twenty-first century. It may well overtake the United States by midcentury. Other developing countries—Brazil and Indonesia, Nigeria and Vietnam—are also likely to see rapid growth. In total, suggests Subramanian, the countries of the developing world will control about two-thirds of global gross domestic product (GDP) as soon as 2030.

This all raises the question: is the United States the next China?

That would be China in the 1850s. A country that crashed from the heights of global economic dominance in a century-long disaster of famine, war, and strife. In the 1850s, China had the largest GDP of any single economy on the planet—a spot it had held for much of the previous four hundred years. The combined wealth of the British Empire had grown considerably larger, however, and it was the British who forced the former top nation into a humiliating series of treaties in the 1860s that made it open its borders to foreign goods—including opium from British India. This was the start of a very bad century for the Far Eastern giant that included civil war, invasion, and mass starvation, all on a colossal scale.

To be fair, even the most depressed pre-mourners for American global power are not quite as gloomy as to predict a resurgence of the Confederacy and civil war, but they do see in China's return to the top spot the risk of US humiliation—forced out of markets and security agreements abroad, in debt bondage to the new superpower at home, the rusting decay of Detroit spreading nationwide. "This time it's different," warned *Financial Times* columnist Gideon Rachman in *Foreign Policy:* "Americans can be forgiven if they greet talk of a new challenge from China as just another case of the boy who cried wolf. But a frequently overlooked fact about that fable is that the boy was eventually proved right. The wolf did arrive—and China is the wolf. China's economic prowess is already allowing Beijing to challenge American influence all over the world."[2]

o o o

THERE IS A MORE OPTIMISTIC alternative. Imagine an America that enjoys its post-imperial might—a retired colossus easing into a big bath of Epsom salts to emerge revived and content. That is the model that Britain followed nine decades after China lost the top spot—when the United Kingdom in turn lost out in heavyweight contention to the United States.

The United States could learn a lot from Britain's experience. Pretending it was still a global power by trying to occupy the

Suez Canal in 1957 topped one of the country's grimmest-ever de-cades—food was still rationed in Britain until 1954, after all. But it was only a year after the Suez Crisis signaled to the world the end of Britain's imperial ambitions that Prime Minister Harold Mac-millan declared that his countrymen had "never had it so good." Certainly, they had never been richer, healthier, or more educated. And after Britain gave up on trying to run an empire and decolo-nized across Africa and Asia in the early 1960s, it got The Beatles, the mini, and free love. Contrast the Ugly American with Austin Powers—really, who was having more fun?

Nowadays the United Kingdom still goes on about "punch-ing above its weight" in international affairs, while the anachro-nistic jollity of its royal family ensures frequent spots on CNN and Star TV. It keeps too many of the trappings of former great-power status, like a seat on the UN Security Council and a small flotilla of nuclear submarines. But freed from the burdens of co-lonial oversight and global leadership, Britain could now retire the two-ocean navy and devalue the pound without the world coming to an end. And Britain could also take an active part in team activities—joining the European Union or signing the Kyoto Accords, for example—without feeling that demeaned its status as above equals. Even better, now that it has managed to import some decent cooking from the bits of the map that used to be pink, the culinary height of a meal out is no longer toad in the hole or spotted dick.

Although the United States shares with Britain and nineteenth-century China the fact that there is little it can do to reverse or even slow its relative global decline, it starts a period of global power transition in a situation far more akin to that of the United King-dom in the twentieth century than of China in the nineteenth. Not least, it is a relatively rich, democratic, and stable country. In fact, it is considerably better off than the United Kingdom was by 1960. It has not exhausted itself in a world war, nor has the economic underpinning of a global empire been dramatically stripped away. And in a good many parts of the United States, it is already possible to find any number of quality restaurants.

o   o   o

NONETHELESS, THE UNITED STATES faces some choices in the decades ahead as to how it is going to act in a new global reality, including how it interacts with the rest of the world. China collapsed too fast in the nineteenth century to have much choice in what followed, but it is fair to say that greater global engagement wasn't part of the strategy. Britain, by contrast, after a rocky start—including a patronizing disdain for Europe that the country could ill afford—embraced its role as a B-list world power with all the enthusiasm of a David Hasselhoff or Paris Hilton. The widespread recognition that Britannia was unlikely ever again to rule more than a few waves and the odd duck pond allowed the country to focus on other things, such as universal health care and Monty Python—much to the benefit of both a domestic population that had paid mightily for its leadership's imperial ambitions and the rest of the world. Britain has emerged as an essential global citizen in areas from development to the environment to peacekeeping.

Again, Europe as a whole, even in the midst of an economic funk, is just an incredibly better place to live and work than it was a half-century ago. Sure, the continent's ability to force its opinions on peoples across the globe has disappeared, and its relative economic weight has been seriously diminished. But choose any measure of the quality of life—health, education, freedom, the quality of public toilets—and things are just so much better than they used to be. Decline and endurance can coexist. In fact, countries in Europe still regularly top the global list in terms of life expectancy, learning, the length of holidays, happiness, innovation, the quality of medieval architecture, siesta length, and all-around wonderfulness. Although Europe may be relegated to a backwater appendage at the left end of the continent that really matters, it could still be in for the time of its life.

And the United States could enjoy exactly the same "decline"—which is in fact an immense upside from dropping down the absolute output rankings. But in order to discover the range of sensible responses the West could have to a changing world economic order, we need to understand the opportunities presented by decline. And that cannot be done without tackling the pessimists' creed as to why the future is going to be grim.

○   ○   ○

FOUR UNQUESTIONED ASSUMPTIONS lie behind the declinists' predictions of misery to come: first, the West is to blame for its own decline; second, biggest is best; third, the rise of the Rest is bad for the West; and finally, fortress America (or fortress Europe) is our only surety. Thus, Charles Krauthammer declares in *The Weekly Standard* that "decline is not a condition. Decline is a choice." He warns that "the international arena remains a Hobbesian state of nature in which countries naturally strive for power," and so, "if we voluntarily renounce much of ours, others will not follow suit. They will fill the vacuum. Inevitably, an inversion of power relations will occur."[3] But it isn't just thinkers from the right who buy into at least some of the declinist agenda. Take Joseph Nye, declaiming from the liberal ramparts of Harvard that "while the 'rise of the rest' means that America will be less dominant than it once was, this does not mean that China will necessarily replace the US as the world's leading power"[4]—as long as the country raises taxes, cuts expenditures, and improves secondary education.

The declinists' prescriptions for Washington or Brussels that follow from these four assumptions are positively harmful for us—and everyone else. Yet despite their support from both left and right, all four assumptions are wrong.

In turn, the first declinist assumption is that our decline is the result of too little investment in education (or roads, or corporate subsidies), or taxation that is too high (or not high enough), or youth who are too addled by television (or fattened by fast food), or old folks who are too coddled by expensive doctors (or financed by federal debt)—name your poison.

But there's good news—this time it really isn't our fault. Chapter 2 lays out the case. The US economy has had some tough years of late, but as a rule it chugs along at a growth rate a little above 2 percent—and has done so ever since hardly anyone went to college, no federal highway system had been built, there were only three channels on TV, and obesity and old folks were both very rare indeed. The heady days of the tech boom at the end of the 1990s saw growth rates maybe half a percent faster than this average. The story is similar for Europe.

Meanwhile, China and India each grew 10 percent in 2011—more than four times our long-term growth rate. The developing world as a whole has an easier time growing fast, because we have invented a lot of technologies they can use to catch up to our levels of wealth. The world is returning to an era when economic dominance is largely a function of population—the default state for humanity for most of history, barring the industrial revolution. So we can stop blaming Washington, or Eurocrats, or kids today, or wastrel boomers for the decline of the West. However annoying they surely are, they are not to blame for China getting bigger than we are. There's one simple reason for that: China has a lot more people than the United States or Europe.

The second verse of the declinist creed praises the benefits of being big. And of course, the United States in particular is a country that thrives on big. From the most powerful military to the largest medal haul at the Olympics, global dominance is part of the American national psyche. So the idea of not being the biggest economy really hurts. Surely the end of economic heavyweight status means even more rapid decline, ever-greater threats to our national security, and a world turned against us.

But big isn't always better—think about the West's own growing problem with obesity. In fact, as Chapter 3 argues, the benefits of being big are much oversold. For a start, being big didn't stop the United States from sliding into recession in 2008, or from sliding down the global league tables—in areas from health to wealth, leisure to liberties, or corruption to incarceration—over the past forty years. And the advantages of brute size in areas from trade to finance to military power are not what they used to be. The World Trade Organization (WTO) constrains trade policy, global financial connections reduce the power of reserve currency status, and imperial adventures are bound by a limited domestic appetite to bear the costs of fighting, combined with a growing global antipathy to wars of conquest. Take the wars in Afghanistan and Iraq, both of which had to be justified as defensive wars to preserve global stability and the public good. There was never any question that the planet's undoubted military hegemon would eventually leave both countries to their own devices. Even better, because those same constraints apply to China, the threat presented to the world by its rising economic hegemony may be limited.

Third up in the declinist litany: pessimists in the West see the rise of the Rest, just like the earlier rise of Japan, as a terrible thing. If the rest of the world gets richer, that means somehow that we in the West must be poorer. One more manufacturing job for China is one less for Louisiana. One more call center employee in Bangalore is one less receptionist in Poughkeepsie. Others fear the rise of the Rest because rich people elsewhere will consume resources as we do—or at least they'll do that until none are left. Having seen the world so recently come off a bubble and plunge into a recession, many find it easy to picture the entire planet ending a resources binge with environmental and economic collapse.

As Chapter 4 suggests, the future is considerably brighter than that. It takes only a few moments' reflection to realize that the concern over economic competition must be, at the very least, overly simplistic, if not completely wrong. If more global wealth really meant a West that is worse off, the United States and Europe would never have been poorer than they are today—because the rest of the world has never been richer. In fact, growing economies overseas are a destination for our exports, a place to invest and a source of investment, and an ever-expanding font of new ideas, technologies, and products that improve the quality of life everywhere. Sure, new industries abroad compete with entrenched interests at home, but they create opportunities for entrepreneurs as well—think of Apple, KFC, and Starbucks selling to all of those newly wealthy Chinese consumers. As long as we help people and companies manage change, global prosperity is great news for the West. And a more peaceful, more cosmopolitan world will be a nicer one to visit, barter with, and live in as well.

But what of concerns about sustainability? Do we have an atmosphere robust enough, or oil wells deep enough, or copper veins broad enough to support a growing global population and its ever-expanding wealth? Will a hotter, more crowded, and massively consuming planet lead to war over resources and environmental collapse? Chapter 5 argues that the challenges are both different and more manageable than this millenarian vision suggests. When it comes to mineral resources in particular, the challenge to the global economy comes not from growing scarcity, but from abundance too great for sustainable use. If we pumped all of the oil out of Canada's tar sands and the rest of the new fossil fuel finds worldwide, we'd toast the planet. Luckily, poor countries are already following a much more sustainable path to wealth than rich countries did in the past.

Again, global prosperity will increase resilience to resource depletion—technology advance creates access to new resources as well as products that require fewer of them. Wealth creates more options for responding to increases in resource prices. There is an undoubted need for an urgent response to the global use of nonrenewables, but the possibility that we will manage to move onto a sustainable growth trajectory is real.

And turning to the final element of the declinist creed, it is not surprising that a nation bruised by two equivocal wars and battered by recession would show signs of surrendering to isolationist tendencies. If the world has no gratitude for American leadership, if the only thing that trade has done for the United States is pile up IOUs to China, if open borders lead only to Mexicans taking our jobs and terrorists and new diseases threatening our lives, it is pretty clear that the rational response is to close the gates and hope the world just goes away.

Except for the fact that the West needs the rest of the world more than ever, as Chapter 6 demonstrates. In an earlier era—sometime before the 1970s—American isolationism might have prolonged the country's status as the largest economy. Today closing off trade, investment, and the flow of people between us and the rest of the world would do harm to them—but more to ourselves.

Take migration: it is all very well to shut the borders, but who's going to pick the fruit and paint the fences? As the West ages, there will be fewer and fewer young, locally born people around to do the heavy lifting. We need to import labor. Meanwhile, the United States in particular could benefit mightily from exporting people—the young to get educated at wholesale prices abroad, adults to find jobs and investment opportunities, and the old to retire in greater comfort with cheaper health care.

Finally, America won't suffer first and it won't suffer the worst from climate change. But when Atlanta in the summer has all the charm of an easy-bake oven and Venice Beach has been re-named Venice Levee, it will be clear why the United States needs to follow Europe and be part of a global solution to environmental concerns. That's just one on a long list of planetary issues that we have to respond to in partnership, because we can't tackle them alone.

o   o   o

NOT ONLY ARE THE FOUR ignoble untruths of declinist belief wrong, but the fact that they are wrong has consequences. On the grounding of this confused worldview is built a set of disastrous policy prescriptions. The idea that we can reverse our decline by ourselves leads to policies that are little more than sandbags against a tsunami of change—and distract us from preparing for a new world. The idea that we'll suffer from the rise of the Rest provokes calls for protection and corporate safety nets that further gum up our economy. The fear of not being biggest encourages outlandish expenditure on maintaining the semblance of leadership—including a US military budget that hides the country's sagging influence as well as a cut-price facelift. And the idea that fortress America or fortress Europe is our only defense impoverishes the West and does considerable harm to the rest of the world. Not least, absent some keen young immigrants, retirement could be a real disappointment for many of us—crabgrass will invade the golf courses and our stock portfolios will shrivel as companies founder for lack of workers.

So how can people in the "old rich" countries benefit from the age of global prosperity by tapping into the greater dynamism of the developing world and ensuring their continued progress? Chapter 7 starts with the opportunities presented by stronger developing economies for individuals in the West. Schooling, work, health care, and retirement opportunities the world over will make it possible for Americans and Europeans, both rich and poor, to enjoy a higher quality of life for less—and to make more money at the same time. While the majority will stay home and do fine despite that, the next thirty years will see the rise of the "global nomad"—born in one country, educated in a second, working in a third, founding a company in a fourth, retiring in a fifth. Here's hoping that, at one point or another in these stages of life, a lot of the new nomads are American and European.

For the US government, suggests Chapter 8, it is time to embrace the benefits of integration. Trade and investment policies should be designed to maximize the benefits of cross-border flows. In a world of global nomads, what matters most is equipping people to succeed wherever they choose to live. Programs from Medicaid to Pell Grants should allow portability of benefits—so that the government and individuals can save money by seeking services abroad.

And given America's mixed success in using brute strength to achieve outcomes, effective bribery through expanded foreign aid might be a cheaper and plausibly more effective substitute. That is especially true given that the largest threat to continued progress for every country, including the United States, is not rogue states but the declining condition of the global environment. Chapter 9 argues that this is another area where America actually needs to increase its global stature by responding to challenges from climate change to declining fisheries stocks and leading by example. Putting taxes and caps on resource usage is an urgent priority. There's also a bigger, better role for the West as a whole to play in eliminating the last pockets of absolute poverty worldwide and meeting global health challenges, from neglected diseases to the threat of antibiotic resistance.

Chapter 10 discusses some of the policies that America in particular might follow to leverage a richer world to ensure the American dream is more than just a dream—where decent health care and a good education guaranteed for every twenty-one-year-old ensure that all kids, however poor or disadvantaged their background, have the opportunity to make it big. Far more than corporate welfare that props up declining industries, investments in people carry the greatest returns in an increasingly globalized economy.

∘ ∘ ∘

THERE'S A DANGER IN purveying a positive message at a time of pessimism—being dismissed as an heir to Pangloss, unable to see the reality of current misery and future catastrophe. Certainly there is enough of the former and risk enough of the latter that both should be repeatedly acknowledged. Fifty percent of the planet's population lives on one-quarter or less of the income that marks the US poverty line. The lives of many of those people—along with those of all too many in the West itself—are made miserable by lack of resources, lack of health, lack of safety, or lack of society. And there are real dangers going forward— from geopolitical tensions to reverses in globalization to rising sea levels and failing crops.

But these risks are *exacerbated* by pessimism and fear. It is those who are concerned by the rise of China who suggest raising the drawbridge—cutting off trade and pumping ever more resources into the military. It is those who would rather see absolute decline twinned with relative stability than relative decline yoked to absolute growth who back weaker global institutions and limited migration. It is those who deny the potential for international agreement who want America to adapt to higher temperatures rather than forge global treaties to avoid them. Pessimism can be a self-fulfilling prophecy, and perhaps the greatest threat to a brighter future is to dwell on the risk of failure. An optimistic view of the future is not only the most plausible; it is also the most helpful. The declinists wallow at their own risk— and ours.

CHAPTER TWO

It's Not Our Fault

THE HISTORIAN ROBERT KAGAN has complained that pundits recently went from America boosting to America bashing in awfully short order. In 2004, he notes, Fareed Zakaria was arguing that the United States enjoyed a "comprehensive unipolarity," and yet only four years later the *Newsweek* editor and CNN host was talking about the "post-American world."[1]

But it isn't just the chattering classes. According to Pew survey evidence across fourteen nations, the percentage of respondents who said that the United States was the leading power in 2010 was still 40 percent—compared to 36 percent who said China. In 2012, China led the United States 42 percent to 36 percent. And while the Chinese themselves don't believe it, American respondents are even more convinced than the global average that their days at the top are over.[2]

As a result, self-flagellation is in the air in America. More specifically, the flagellation of Washington is in the air. Why is the country on the skids, falling behind, destined to be a second-rate power? Blame Congress. And the president. And (always) the East Coast Media Elite.

Talking of whom, take the 2011 tome by Thomas Friedman and Michael Mandelbaum, *That Used to Be Us*. The subtitle is *How America Fell Behind in the World It Invented, and How We Can Come Back*. They advocate entitlement reform, alternative energy investments, and faster subway escalator repair as key to America's renaissance.[3] Meanwhile, Niall Ferguson argues in his book *Civilization* that the West led over the Rest because of six "killer apps"—competition, science, property, medicine, consumption, and work. The Rest has now downloaded these apps, suggests Ferguson, but if the United States reboots the software, it can upgrade its civilization. Not that it has been doing too well at that, he thinks: under President Obama, America is "a superpower in retreat, if not retirement."[4]

To which the answer is: well, sort of. Surely Washington could do a lot better at running the country. Not least, as Ferguson suggests, it could do something about special interest lobbying, and a (still) dysfunctional health care system. And as Friedman and Mandelbaum make clear, more infrastructure and education investment alongside stricter energy standards would surely help. But the idea that if only Washington started to act, well, more *Washingtonian* the United States could remain top nation is still silly. Indeed, Ferguson at times admits that "the Chinese Century" is somewhat of a foregone conclusion. Whatever we do to improve the functioning of the US economy, the idea that we can outrun China or India for long is just wishful thinking.

The relative economic decline of the United States is not about gridlock in Washington, stupidity or venality on Wall Street, the lack of can-do spirit among the young, or even the death of "the Greatest Generation." It is about the rest of the world finally getting its act together. That's not to say that America is doing everything right, of course; much of the rest of this book is about what the country could do better to engage with a new world of opportunity. But it is important to recognize that policies to "regain US dominance" are destined to fail—and are likely to be counterproductive.

○ ○ ○

FOR MOST OF THE LAST two hundred years, the story of global incomes has been one of the rich getting richer and the poor staying poor—or "divergence, big time," as Harvard's Lant Pritchett puts it.[5] In 1870 the world's richest country was probably about nine times as rich as the poorest country. By 1990 that gap had increased to a forty-five-fold difference. And populations had grown fast in many of the stagnant economies at the wrong end of this divergence. As a result, the number of the "absolute poor" worldwide—those living on $1.25 a day or less—had climbed dramatically. In 1981, 1.9 billion people, or half of the population of the developing world, lived in absolute poverty, according to Shaohua Chen and Martin Ravallion of the World Bank. At this level of destitution, obtaining adequate nutrition just to survive would take up the great majority of a person's resources—leaving precious little for shelter, medical care, or anything else.[6]

But since then, the pattern has reversed. In the 1980s, the average GDP per capita growth rate in developing countries was 1.4 percent, according to data from the World Bank. In the 1990s, that climbed to 1.8 percent. In the first decade of the new century, the number shot up to 4.4 percent—considerably higher than growth rates in rich countries.[7] As a result, a lot of countries formerly known as "developing" are looking considerably better off nowadays. Few would argue that Italy and Austria were not "developed" economies in 1960. And yet average incomes not just in China but in Mexico, Thailand, Russia, Malaysia, and Argentina (among others) are considerably higher today than they were in Italy or Austria in 1960.

Meanwhile, incomes per head in the United States, the United Kingdom, Germany, and Japan increased by around 1 percent a year over the past decade. The US economy expanded in size by 18 percent from 2000 to 2010, ahead of the United Kingdom (15 percent) and Germany and Japan (less than 10 percent). In a ranking of the 164 countries for which the World Bank has data on GDP growth over the decade, the United States came in 134th, with the United Kingdom, Germany, and Japan in 140th, 154th, and 155th place. At the same time, the top nineteen countries in the world in growth over the decade—all of which were developing countries—saw their GDPs more than *double* over the ten years from 2000 to 2010. And that top nineteen included some really big countries—not least India and China— so nearly 2.6 billion people benefited from all of that economic dynamism.[8]

But this isn't just a story of leaping Chinese tigers and waking Indian elephants—even Africa, traditionally written off as a hopeless economic backwater, has joined in the progress. That continent has been growing like gangbusters, though you probably haven't noticed, because the forty-nine African countries still have a combined economy smaller than Texas at market exchange rates.[9] The club of economies that doubled in size included no fewer than eight from Africa south of the Sahara. Indeed, sub-Saharan Africa took seventeen out of the top forty spots in the decade's global GDP growth rankings. Although populations have expanded since 2000—by around 28 percent—the fact that the region's GDP is now 66 percent larger than it was in 2000 still suggests that the average income in the region is about one-third higher than it was ten years ago.[10]

In turn, we have seen a dramatic fall in the number of the world's absolutely destitute. From 1.9 billion people in 1981, the number of people living on $1.25 a day or less worldwide fell to around 1.3 billion in 2005, according to estimates from Laurence Chandy and Geoffrey Gertz of the Brookings Institution. And they suggest that the number was below 900 million in 2010. They estimate that the proportion of people living in absolute poverty has shrunk from one-half of the developing world in 1981 to less than one-sixth today.[11]

o o o

THE REAL QUESTION FOR the relative standing of the West and the Rest, and for the absolute quality of life of people worldwide, is this: will the countries of the developing world continue to follow the pattern of the last fifteen years, or will they revert to the long-term pattern of stagnation? After all, even though the rapid growth of newly independent developing countries in the 1960s set them on a convergence course with incomes in the rich world of the era, this growth petered out soon thereafter. Nothing is preordained.

Part of the answer to this question depends on what underlies the wealth of nations. First, is it people, or is it place? Are certain parts of humanity just incapable of generating wealth, or is it something in the nature of the societies they live in—or the geography of their surroundings—that keeps them poor? And if it is about place rather than people, is it a feature that is easy to change or one that has persisted over centuries, dooming some countries to perpetual economic disappointment?

The debate about people over place is one that richer people have about poorer people across town and across the planet: Why are they poor? Is it circumstances, or is it some kind of moral or intellectual failing on the part of individuals? Is it that poor people never had a *chance* to cross from the wrong to the right side of the tracks, or that they never had the *motivation* to cross?

Some believe that the poor in America would be better off if only they weren't so lackadaisical about work, or if only they weren't so congenitally stupid. This view colors their thinking about international development as well. But in fact, poverty in Africa and Asia isn't the result of something about individual Kenyans and Pakistanis, it is instead something about Kenya and Pakistan. Individuals the world over have the same drives and capacities, but the societies and places in which they live present radically different opportunities to turn that drive into wealth, health, and well-being.

That's clear from evidence compiled by Princeton economist Orley Ashenfelter for the National Bureau of Economic Research. He looks at the wages earned by staff working at McDonald's franchises around the world and compares what they earn to the cost of a Big Mac in that same franchise. The Big Mac is a standard product, and the way it is made worldwide is highly standardized. The skill level involved in making it (such as it is) is the same everywhere. And yet McDonald's employees worldwide earn dramatically different amounts in terms of Big Macs per hour.[12]

In the United States, a McDonald's employee earns an average of $7.22 an hour, and a Big Mac costs an average of $3.04. So the employee earns 2.4 Big Macs per hour. In India, an employee earns $.46 an hour. The average Indian Big Mac (made of chicken, which is cheaper than beef) costs only $1.29. Still, the employee earns only one-third of a Big Mac for each hour worked. Same job, same skills—and yet Indian workers at McDonald's earn one-seventh the real hourly wage of a US employee. There's a huge "place premium" to working in the United States rather than India.

The place premium affects more than just low-end service jobs. Economist Michael Clemens, a colleague of mine at the Center for Global Development, studied a group of Indians working in an India-based international software firm who applied for a temporary work visa to the United States to do the same work in the same firm, just on the other side of the Pacific Ocean. Some of them then won the lottery by which visas were issued, while others lost. The winning workers, who were still in the same firm and still doing the same type of job on the same projects, suddenly saw dramatic differences in their pay. The ones who moved to the United States started earning double what their colleagues back in India were earning (adjusted for purchasing power). They were earning more *not* because they were different from the colleagues they left behind—selection was not based on education, talent, or drive but was entirely random. And once they returned to India, they went back to earning pretty much the same as their colleagues who had never left. They briefly earned more in the United States simply because they were in the United States rather than India. Clemens concludes that location alone—the place premium—accounts for three-quarters of the difference in average pay levels between software workers in the United States and their counterparts in India. That leaves different production technology and levels of effort accounting for a maximum of one-quarter of the wage difference altogether.[13]

So the overwhelming explanation for who is rich and who is poor on a global scale isn't about *who* you are, but *where* you are. And why do very similar people in the United States earn so much more doing the exact same jobs as people in India? The answer lies in *infrastructure*—physical infrastructure like (comparatively) good road and electricity networks alongside economic infrastructure, including a (somewhat) robust banking system—and *institutions,* such as a (passable) set of commercial laws and (not completely capricious) regulatory regimes. The higher quality of these public goods allows the same amount of effort by the same-quality employee to create considerably more value in the United States than in India.

But when we move from the question of people or place to the question "Why does the United States have superior institutions?" or "Are those features of place easy to change?" we see that many of the foremost thinkers in the field of development economics are busy digging through the history books—and suggesting that institutions are very deep-rooted indeed.

More than a decade ago, MIT's Daron Acemoglu and Simon Johnson, authors of the economics blockbuster *Why Nations Fail,* published a paper with another colleague, James Robinson, showing that areas where colonists lived long and healthy lives in the nineteenth century (think North America and Australia) went on to become rich countries at the close of the twentieth century. Meanwhile, areas like Africa and the Caribbean where early colonists died in large numbers, succumbing to tropical diseases like malaria and yellow fever, are today far poorer countries. The reason, argue Acemoglu and Johnson, is that where only a small elite of colonists survived disease, societies were very unequal and colonial authorities had little incentive—or even had a positive disincentive—to provide public services like health and education to the mass of the population. Conversely, in areas that colonists could stay healthy in and occupy en masse (often wiping out local peoples in the process), the societies that developed were far more equal.[14]

Acemoglu, Johnson, and Robinson's work set off a race to dig further into the past to uncover statistical associations between historical characteristics and modern income. By 2006, we'd gone back three millennia. When New York University's Bill Easterly and his colleagues asked, "Was the Wealth of Nations Determined in 1000 BC?," they discovered that areas with technologies like writing, pottery, forging, wheeled vehicles, agriculture, and iron weapons back then developed into richer countries three thousand years later.[15]

This makes for grim reading, at least at first glance. It suggests that who is rich and who is poor is determined by centuries or millennia of history, which in turn is related to which countries developed strong institutions of government to provide quality public services and which countries did not. This is a very long process. The corollary idea is that places that are poor today are likely to remain poor for a long time. Perhaps the recent good news out of Asia, Africa, and the rest of the developing world is just a temporary aberration. Just as strong growth in the 1960s petered out into sputtering performance in the 1970s and '80s, perhaps the next twenty years will see renewed stagnation in the global South.

The depressing nature of the deep-institutions-as-destiny theory of the wealth and poverty of nations lies behind perhaps the most audacious—if failed—development experiment of the recent past: the Honduran government's decision to set up a "charter city" on the country's eastern coast. The brainchild of New York University economist Paul Romer, the charter city would have had considerable independence from Honduras's own institutions of government. It would have been overseen by an international body of eminent economists and development practitioners, with a judicial system topped by the Mauritius High Court half a world away and constitutional protection from interference from Honduras's parliament. The country's own Supreme Court blocked the idea, and Romer has withdrawn from the project. But the concept was that if institutions are the secret to success, and Honduras's institutions don't work now and are unlikely to work for a long time, the solution is to carve out a bit of the country and import some working institutions from elsewhere to operate it. Think of it as a Hong Kong for the twenty-first century.

Luckily for Hondurans denied their charter city—and more broadly for the developing world as a whole—there's a more optimistic way to read the record of economic history. While *where* you are is a powerful predictor of your *relative* wealth, health, and education, *when* you are is at least as powerful a predictor of your *absolute* wealth, health, and education. And that suggests the potential for widespread—and continued—progress in incomes and quality of life worldwide.

Thirty years ago, Richard Easterlin gave a presidential address to the Economic History Association asking, "Why Isn't the Whole World Developed?," which made the case for this more optimistic version of future history. His answer to the question was that economic growth is the result of the spread of knowledge about how to use production technologies, from the steam engine to the assembly line. And fundamental to the wide spread of that knowledge is broad-based education. The richest countries in the modern world were those where basic education had become widespread earliest, but poor countries would catch up, he noted, as education spread.[16]

To some extent, Easterlin's analysis jibes with the more recent work of scholars from Acemoglu to Easterly. After all, those countries where education was close to universal in the nineteenth century are also countries that had happier colonial histories or that discovered the compass earlier. But the conclusion that Easterlin drew for the future of poor countries was far more positive. He noted that education was rapidly spreading across the developing world and that this spread had been accompanied by "the diffusion of modern economic growth." He predicted that, as countries completed a "demographic transition" to low birthrates and long lives toward the end of the twentieth century, "their long-term growth rates will be at least as high as those that the developed countries have so far experienced."[17]

The economic historian was right about trends in health and education. Life expectancies have climbed thirty years in China since 1960 and twenty-three years in India, according to World Bank data. And rates of enrollment in secondary education have gone from 37 to 60 percent in India and from 38 to 80 percent in China over the two decades since 1990. Pretty much everywhere else in the developing world has followed suit. In 1990 nearly 12 million children worldwide died before they reached their fifth birthday. By 2010 that figure was below 8 million.[18] And of all the people in human history who ever reached the age of sixty-five, half are alive now, reflecting considerably improved global trends in adult health as well. Again, contemporary populations of countries such as Haiti, Zambia, and Bangladesh have spent more time in school on average than the populations of France, Germany, and Spain as recently as 1970.[19]

Still, Easterlin's forecast had a rough couple of decades. In the twenty years after his 1981 lecture, developing countries continued to improve health and education access, yet growth rates declined across Africa and Latin America, significantly lagging behind the West.[20] The cross-country link between education and economic performance appeared so weak that the Harvard economist Lant Pritchett wrote a much-cited paper asking "Where Has All the Education Gone?"[21]

But we have seen that as the last century drew to a close, growth rates in the developing world did finally pick up, as Easterlin had suggested they would. And perhaps that growth really is linked to improved institutions and public services. Because even a lot of countries that saw high mortality among colonists or that lacked wheeled vehicles in 1000 BC are providing some government services today, not just education (even in sub-Saharan Africa, more than three-quarters of primary-age children are enrolled in school) but also health care; four-fifths of all children even in low-income countries (those with a GDP per capita of around $1,000 or less) are vaccinated against measles, for example. That's one reason why today's life expectancy in the former British colony of Ghana is about twenty-three years higher than in imperial Britain itself back in 1850.[22] And even basic democratic rights have spread— long-term measures of levels of democracy kept by George Mason University suggest that the world has never been as democratic as it is today.[23]

Of course, governments across the developing world could still do a lot better in providing the services that may underpin economic advance. Take education: the vast majority of kids worldwide may graduate from primary school, but all too many leave knowing not too much more than they did when they arrived. More than one-third of African children who complete their primary education haven't mastered basic literacy or numeracy by the time they leave.[24] In health care services, survey evidence from India suggests that the average number of questions asked in an appointment with a government doctor in the country is one, which amounts to "What's wrong with you?"[25] Again, when it comes to the rule of law, it's hardly reassuring that about half of the people surveyed by Transparency International in sub-Saharan Africa report having paid a bribe to a government official sometime over the previous twelve months.[26]

But the fact remains: the average developing country sees a quality and reach of government services that would have astounded the citizens of many rich countries only a century ago—long after Western economies had started their sustained progress toward high wealth. If the quality of government institutions really is the secret to future riches, the global economy—and in particular the world's poorest people—could be in for a great few decades.

Perhaps as a result, even proponents of deep-rooted determinants of development are getting more optimistic about global convergence. For example, Enrico Spolaore and Romain Wacziarg of the National Bureau of Economic Research suggest that "genetic distance"—a measure of when two populations share common ancestors—predicts present-day economic outcomes. The smaller the genetic distance between two populations, the more similar their modern incomes. Spolaore and Wacziarg suggest that this happens because genetically closer populations also share similar cultural values, which in turn are linked to the quality of institutions and the ease with which new approaches and technologies can be adopted across borders. At the same time, Spolaore and Wacziarg note that culture is less of a barrier to development than it used to be. They suggest that genetic proximity has around half of the influence on income differences today as it did in 1870, now accounting for only about one-third of cross-country income differences. Going forward, that proportion may well drop further thanks to the globalization of ideas, convergence in norms, and spreading education.[27]

o o o

SO HISTORY ALONE does not necessarily *condemn* the developing world to a slowdown, but that does not mean growth will continue. Indeed, if the past is any guide, growth almost certainly won't continue in some places. Twenty years ago, economists Bill Easterly, Michael Kremer, Lant Pritchett, and Larry Summers—with research support from current Facebook chief operating officer Sheryl Sandberg—wrote a paper on the drivers of long-term growth. They pointed out that strong performance in one decade is hardly related to fast growth in the next. In fact, there is almost no relationship between the relative speed of country growth rates over time. Just as with mutual funds, past performance is no guarantee of future success. The paper (titled "Good Policy or Good Luck?") concluded that growth "miracles" are, in fact, largely good luck. That's one more nail in the coffin of expectations for growth that rely on hundreds of years of history.[28]

This conclusion also suggests that anyone willing to forecast future growth rates had better be ready, of course, to wipe a lot of egg off his or her face. It has been only a quarter-century, for example, since corporate strategist Kenichi Ohmae was predicting the Triad—a world economy led by the United States, Europe, and Japan. The more optimistic of the Euro-boosters was predicting a "European Century" even more recently than that. Today, the United States is perhaps the most stable leg of Ohmae's Triad, but no global economic system would feel too secure sitting on that stool right now.[29]

With that by way of considerable caveat, what might the future hold for the economic fortunes of the Rest? Take China, a country that has grown at a little over 8 percent a year for over thirty years. Can it manage the same trick for another decade or two? There are lots of reasons to worry. Growth slowed in 2011–2012 and was forecast to dip below 8 percent in 2013. Increased lending during this period of slower growth might be a sign of lower returns to investment, perhaps related to evidence of real estate bubbles in a number of Chinese cities—all of which contributes to fears that China's biggest banks are carrying (although not yet reporting) a growing stock of bad debt, feeding into longer-term concerns that the country is due for a full-on banking crisis.

Cleaning up the financial sector is just one of a set of adjustments that many officials in China and many economists in the rest of the world suggest is necessary if China's growth is to continue. Hongmei Yi, Linxui Zhang, and their colleagues from the Chinese Academy of Sciences point out that many Chinese children remain so excluded from the opportunities of future growth as to be a significant drag on economic performance. During the last ten years, fewer than half of kids in poor rural areas of China matriculated to high school. Many of those children suffered debilitating conditions: as many as half of those from the poorer surveyed counties were anemic, and one-fifth were infected with roundworms.[30]

And Raghuram Rajan, former economic counselor at the International Monetary Fund and now India's central bank governor, noted some time ago that over the longer term, China would have to move away from a growth model based heavily on ev-er-greater exports to one based more on domestic demand for goods and services. In turn, the savings rate would have to be re-duced from its current level of about half of GDP, and the artifi-cially low exchange rate would have to be abandoned in order to allow China's currency, the renminbi, to float. Zhu Min, deputy managing director of the IMF, has even argued that a slowdown would be helpful to China because it would give Beijing space to move to that new model.[31]

But Harvard economist Dani Rodrik estimates that if China revalued its currency as part of an effort to reorient the econ-omy, a 20 percent appreciation might reduce China's growth rate by nearly two percentage points.[32] And more broadly, there is no consensus over the overall policy package needed to sustain output growth. If economic liberalization is a prerequisite, for example, the country has a long way to go. The World Bank sug-gests that China ranks 151st out of 183 economies in terms of how easily the official steps required to set up a new business can be followed. But of course, China's astounding economic perfor-mance of the last twenty years was hardly driven by an orthodox prescription of free markets, free exchange rates, and mass pri-vatization, so it isn't clear that suddenly adopting that strategy is a sensible policy.[33]

More optimistically, economic historian and Nobel laureate Robert Fogel has argued that there is certainly the potential for China to continue growing at 8 percent until 2030. There are still opportunities for more adults to work despite an aging popula-tion. And labor is likely to move into more productive sectors over time—out of agriculture into manufacturing and services. These two factors alone could account for 30 percent of the country's continued growth, Fogel suggests.[34] Similarly, Rodrik, who is bearish on the subject of future growth miracles in general and at best neutral on China, still suggests that manufacturing industries in the developing world see productivity converge with the globally most efficient firms in their sector at the rate of about 3 percent per year, "regardless of policies, institutions, or geography." That's good news for China—because manufacturing accounts for nearly one-third of the country's GDP.[35]

Again, there are considerable opportunities to increase labor productivity through education. Between 1990 and 2004, China's college enrollment rate increased sixfold, but it is still far below Western levels, suggesting that space exists for continued catch-up. And at least in Shanghai the schools are pretty good: the city's scores in the Program for International Student Assessment for fifteen-year-olds in math, science, and reading were higher than the average for any country tested. At the tertiary level, eighteen Chinese universities make it onto a list of the world's top five hundred (in a compilation by Shanghai University, which might be biased, of course).[36] If China achieves universal secondary enrollment and, by 2025, reaches the levels of college and university enrollment achieved by Western European nations in the 1980s, Fogel suggests, that might add more than 6 percent to growth rates.[37] That prediction may be too optimistic given that current graduates are having trouble finding jobs. Nonetheless, the fact that it can be made is a sign of China's potential for continued rapid growth.

And even if there are as many plausible arguments as to why China's growth should slow as there are plausible arguments that it will continue, it is worth noting that even the more pessimistic forecasts of China's long-term potential would be considered hopelessly *optimistic* for most countries. In 2010 the Asian Development Bank projected that China could grow at a 5.5 percent annual average over the two decades to 2030, although if it improved education, research, and property rights, that might climb to 6.6 percent. If China's income growth slowed to 5.5 percent, its income per capita (at purchasing power parity) would still be around $33,000 by 2030—up from around $11,000 in 2010 and about the same as the European Union average in that year. At these growth rates, the Chinese economy will be about twice the size of the US economy in 2030. So even with a slowdown, the Asian Century looks like a foregone conclusion.[38]

A similar story of potential slowdown but reasons for optimism can be told about the rest of the developing world. As Harvard's Dani Rodrik points out in his influential paper "The Future of Convergence," there are plenty of reasons to expect that the experience of the last decade was the exception and that soon enough we will go back to a world of stagnating incomes in many poor countries. He argues that growth is likely to be sustained only if the bulk of those countries can manage to foster structural transformation that puts more and more of their workers in manufacturing and some segments of service industries. And many countries achieving that transformation all at once—especially when most have signed up to WTO free-trading rules that limit the scope for subsidizing local export industries in their infancy—might be very hard. For example, India's recent growth has not relied on China's model of manufacturing exports, but rather on domestic demand and services exports. There has not yet been a country that has made it rich on that exact model.[39]

At the same time, others view the potential for growth in a world of open trade more positively. Richard Baldwin, writing for the National Bureau of Economic Research, argues that the barriers to industrialization have dropped dramatically over the past couple of decades because of the spread of international production chains: a single product (like the iPhone) is designed in one country and assembled in another out of parts from a third, fourth, and fifth country, using raw materials from a bunch of other places. Thus, a country doesn't have to become an efficient producer in all parts of the industrial process at once, but only in one stage of production, to become a manufacturing power-house. "No nation today produces all the parts and components necessary to make aircraft, cars or electronics," Baldwin notes. Instead, the value chain for a final product passes through many countries. Low transport costs, reduced tariffs, and the ease of international coordination thanks to new communications tech-nologies have combined to make it possible to assemble a final product from widgits made elsewhere in turn based on doodads from even farther afield.[40]

Twentieth-century trade, suggests Baldwin, was primarily about selling "goods made in factories in one nation to custom-ers in another." In the twenty-first century, trade is increasingly about "two-way flows of people, training, investment, and in-formation that used to take place within factories and offices."[41] The Chinese content of the country's "processing exports" is less than 20 percent, and these exports account for more than half of the nation's boom in manufacturing trade. That's of huge benefit to the United States and the West, of course—overall, it makes for cheaper iPads and laptops, where much of the profit accrues to US inputs, including design. But these "two-way flows" also make it easier for entrepreneurs in other developing countries to get into the export business.

There is even continued hope for Africa. As it enters its own demographic transition, its dependent-to-worker ratio (the number of kids and old people compared to the size of the working-age population) will rapidly drop. And even though the quality of schooling is generally very low, the region will benefit from a workforce that has been exposed to almost universal primary education and considerable secondary and tertiary education—in other words, education levels that are far higher than in the West at similar income levels. Democracy has been stabilizing across much of the continent, and innovations from biometric identification to contract publication are slowly improving the quality of regional governance. It is quite possible that firms on the continent will start joining international production chains in large enough numbers to sustain rapid growth.

○ ○ ○

MEANWHILE, WHATEVER THE REASON for *poor* countries at last starting to act as theories of economic growth have long said they should, we'll see that *big* economies have never been graced with particularly impressive growth rates, and there's no particular reason to think they should suddenly start growing faster today. So America is unlikely to see an 8 percent growth spurt anytime soon—whoever controls Congress and the executive branch. And even if the Euro Zone finally manages to agree on a permanent solution to the conundrum of currency union among sovereign states, Europe won't grow much faster. Two and a half percent is about the long-term average, and it is likely to remain so. The developing world is forecast to grow at twice that rate or more.

So let's assume for the moment that convergence continues, even if at a less breakneck pace than in the recent past. What does that suggest about the future, and where will convergence lead the world? As long as China continues to grow at a reasonable rate, it will soon eclipse both the United States and the European Union. India will follow. And the rise of these two nations suggests a return to the past. For millennia, the measure of a state's success was land and population—think of the biblical celebration that "the children of Israel were fruitful, and increased abundantly, and multiplied, and waxed exceeding mighty; and the land was filled with them." As incomes converge, population will return as the ultimate arbiter of economic power.

By 2030, the UN predicts, there will be around 8.3 billion people living worldwide. India will be the world's most populous country by that point, followed by China. These two countries between them will account for one-third of the world's population. India alone will be home to about three times as many people as currently live in the countries of the European Union, and more than four times as many people as there now are in the United States.[42]

And the dominance of these countries will not be solely based on brute numbers—Asia's (and Africa's) populations will also be younger. According to UN projections, 35 percent of North America's population, and 29 percent of Europe's, will be under thirty years old in 2030. That compares to 42 percent in Asia and Latin America and 62 percent in Africa. Between 2009 and 2050, UN population forecasts suggest, developing regions will add 1.5 billion to their workforces while the workforce in the developed world will actually *shrink* by 100 million as aging reduces the proportion of the working-age population from 63 percent to 52 percent of the citizenry.

Converging productivity and growing workforces in the developing world will return the planet to a state of global economic dominance by the Rest. In 1500, Brazil, India, Indonesia, and China between them accounted for 51 percent of the world's population and 52 percent of the world's output, according to Arvind Subramanian. In 1960 they still made up 42 percent of the world's population, but only 12 percent of world GDP. By 2030, the world may be back closer to parity: the three countries sharing 42 percent of the world's population will account for 40 percent of global GDP.[43]

Subramanian predicts that by 2030 the world will have four major economic players. China will be the heavyweight, with a share of global GDP around 24 percent (measured at purchasing power parity). Next will be India, the European Union, and the United States—each with 10 to 12 percent of global output. Brazil, Indonesia, and Japan will each control a little more than 3 percent of global GDP.[44]

Subramanian is not the only one who sees the world that way. Uri Dadush of the Carnegie Endowment suggests that by 2050, Brazil, China, Indonesia, India, Mexico, and Russia will have a combined economy of $80 trillion—larger than the economies of the combined G-7 nations (the United States, the United Kingdom, France, Germany, Italy, Canada, and Japan) and more than double the size of the whole world's economy in 2009.[45] Meanwhile, according to the forecasts of the accounting firm PricewaterhouseCoopers, even using fairly conservative long-term growth rates, India may be nearly as large as the United States by 2050, Brazil's economy will be larger than Japan's, Indonesia and Mexico will have bigger GDPs than Germany or the United Kingdom, and the Turkish economy might be the same size as Italy's.[46]

But all of these different forecasts also suggest that *everyone*—both the Rest and the West—will be richer. For example, PricewaterhouseCoopers estimates suggest that average incomes in the United States in 2050 will be around $93,000, compared to $44,000 in 2007. Germany and the United Kingdom will both see average incomes above $70,000. The average Mexican in 2050 will be richer than the average US citizen today, and Chinese average incomes will be above Germany's today, at $35,000.[47]

There are good reasons, then, to think that developing country growth will continue to outstrip Western growth rates, even if not so dramatically as in the last decade. Even conservative forecasts imply that the future world economy will no longer be dominated by the countries bordering the Atlantic and that the Pacific Century is firmly entrenched. But even conservative forecasts also suggest that the countries bordering the Atlantic will be richer than ever too. The world's center of gravity will have shifted, but *everywhere* will be better off for that.

o o o

SO THE RELATIVE RISE of the Rest is likely to continue, and not primarily because of Western idiocy. None of this is to suggest that Washington and Wall Street (or Brussels and Frankfurt) are as innocent as newborn lambs. The collective incompetent greed of bankers out to make a buck on mortgage roulette, combined with regulators and politicians desperate to backstop their irresponsible gambling, undoubtedly helped cause the global financial crisis of 2007–2008. But over the long term, not even the considerable inadequacies of New York and Washington are powerful enough to explain what is occurring in the global economy, and that, frankly, should come as a relief to the rest of America—which was apparently idiot enough to give its money to one lot and its votes to the other.

Having said that, there are lots of ways in which America is falling behind that *are* its fault—in child health, education, and inequality, for example. Europe, too, is seeing a declining quality of life in a number of dimensions. For both America and Europe, however, there is a space for policies to leverage the rise of the Rest to reverse those declines, the subject of later chapters. Here, the good news is that one thing that doesn't matter to broader quality of life is absolute economic scale. Biggest by no means equals best.

CHAPTER THREE

Biggest Doesn't Equal Best

T HE ARGUMENT BOILS BETWEEN "declinists" and "endurists" as to the state of America. "American Decline: This Time It's for Real," argued Gideon Rachman in *Foreign Policy*. "China's Century? Why America's Edge Will Endure," reported Michael Beckley in *International Security*. "Empire Falls," warned Robert Pape in *National Interest*—only a year after *American Interest* carried Edward Luttwak's "The Declinists, Wrong Again." The list goes on.[1]

And, in part, the argument continues because writers—or at least the editors who title their articles—are arguing past each other. As already pointed out, relative *economic* decline for the United States implies neither *absolute* decline in anything nor loss of leadership in areas from cultural influence to quality of life to the global reach of a country's drone strikes.

Still, the majority of the American public appears to be concerned about the country's relative economic decline even more than its absolute level of income or quality of life. According to a 2012 Chicago Council Survey, 40 percent of Americans view China's economy growing as large as the US economy as "mostly negative," compared to 9 percent who view it as "mostly positive." Sixty percent of Americans, according to a recent YouGov poll, prefer a scenario where America's income increases only 10 percent but the country's economy remains larger than China's to one where the US economy doubles in size but China's economy nonetheless overtakes it to become the largest in the world.[2]

Focusing on gross output as a measure of national status—let alone national quality of life—is just terribly twentieth-century. Being the biggest economy isn't all that important. Sure, controlling the world's reserve currency is nice, and having a military big enough to crush any potential invasion is cool. But neither of these benefits has stopped America's decline into mediocrity among rich countries when it comes to measures of social inequality, crime, health, and education. There's just not much of a relationship between having the largest economy and faster economic growth or higher quality of life. On the flip side, for all China is already the largest economy on some measures, the quality of life of the average person in the Middle Kingdom is nowhere near as high as in the United States. And just as important, China as the top economy poses little threat to the global economic system or US national security.

o   o   o

CHINA'S GROWING GLOBAL PROMINENCE extends beyond simple measures of output. Although the United States and the European Union both had shares of world trade more than four times larger than China's as recently as 2000, by 2010 their shares were all within a percentage point of each other (and by 2012 China was in the lead). Again, China accounted for only 4 percent of world net capital exports in 2000, but this had climbed to 18 percent by 2010. The United States, meanwhile, accounted for more than half of net capital *imports* as by far the world's biggest debtor nation.[3]

We have seen that in 2030, China is likely to account for about one-quarter of world GDP, compared to 12 percent for the United States. It will account for 15 to 20 percent of world trade, compared to 7 percent each for the United States and the European Union forecasts Arvind Subramanian. China's share of global trade and GDP will look similar to US shares in 1950, and its net capital exports share will be similar to that of the United States in 1973.

Pessimists warn that being knocked off the top spot in terms of output, trade, and finance might have all sorts of ill effects for the US economy. For a start, most of the world's central banks—the Bank of England, the European Central Bank, and the People's Bank of China, among them—hold large stocks of dollars in their electronic vaults as reserves. The dollar is the preferred currency of trade, and commodities such as oil are priced in US currency. But the dollar's share in global reserves has already fallen from around 80 percent to below 40 percent since the mid-1970s, replaced not least by the euro and by China's renminbi. The cable news network CNBC recently splashed a report featuring fund managers who suggested that "the number-one security issue we have as a nation is the preservation of the US dollar as the world's reserve currency." If the dollar loses status, they warned, "the United States will lose the right to print money to pay its debt. It will be forced to pay this debt."

It is quite possible that China's currency, the renminbi, will take over the dollar's status as the world's reserve currency and be used by central banks and trading companies to pay international debts. And there is a real fear that a newly dominant China could throw its weight around if it controls a growing portion of world trade along with the reserve currency of choice. After all, the United States itself used its economic dominance to boss around other countries to its own advantage, including breaking numerous international commitments by suspending the convertibility of the dollar into gold and imposing a 10 percent import surcharge as a means to persuade partner countries to revalue their currencies in 1971. That retreat toward protectionism combined with the oil crises to put the global economy into a funk for much of the 1980s.

But even the combination of being both big and rich, along with holding the favored reserve currency, didn't do the United States all that much good in terms of strengthening economic performance over the past century, and it won't do China much good either. Indeed, between 1890, when the United States overtook China as the world's largest economy, and 2008, when China was about to return to the top spot, China's annualized income per capita growth was about one-quarter of a percentage point *higher* than in the United States. US growth performance over those 118 years ranked fifteenth out of thirty-seven countries for which we have data, behind economies that included Denmark, Canada, Sweden, and (even) Greece. Even a number of *really small* countries have done better than America. Luxembourg has a GDP that is four-tenths of a percent the size of the US economy, about the same output as the state of Delaware. Yet, despite its teeny GDP, it is more than twice as rich per person as the United States. Other things being equal, being *rich* makes you grow more slowly on average—and the evidence that being *big* necessarily makes you grow faster is very weak indeed.[4]

If the dollar does lose reserve status, Americans may have to pay a little more to borrow money abroad and will face the costs of currency exchange to buy foreign goods. But overseas firms already have to hedge currency risk and still manage to compete, while recent evidence suggests that there's no imminent need to worry that speculators are going to force up the cost of US borrowing despite the slipping status of the dollar—in fact, the interest rate on federal government debt hadn't been as low as it was in 2013 for more than a century.

Even if China tries to use its economic size to its advantage— as it surely will—by manipulating exchange rates or throwing up tariffs, thanks in no small part to the global financial and trading system that the United States helped to create, the new economic hegemon's room for maneuver will be considerably constrained.

If the renminbi is to become a global reserve currency, for example, China will have to develop financial markets that are deep, liquid, and open to foreigners. At the moment, money can't flow freely into and out of the country and China's financial markets can't match the scale and complexity of Wall Street. There are signs that the government is responding to some of these challenges—not least, it has started to allow trades in renminbi. Further steps in that direction—which would involve the devaluation of the renminbi—would increase the export competitiveness of the rest of the world's goods as well as create an exciting investment opportunity for those few in the rich world still actually saving money.

Furthermore, China will become the dominant economic power in a period when the international trading regime appears to have weathered the threat of a retreat behind tariff walls—a threat that doomed the last great period of globalization, ending with the Great Depression. For all there hasn't been a new world trade agreement, countries are abiding by the rules of the treaties already signed and responding when the World Trade Organization calls them out for misbehavior. That includes China: after a complaint to the WTO by the United States and others, a WTO ruling forced China to drop export taxes on a number of raw materials, including bauxite and zinc, in 2012. China will also become the biggest trader while still an economy benefiting from "catch-up" growth, which involves exploiting tools and processes developed in rich countries and responding to the demand for a level of openness to global finance and technology.

In fact, China is already a far more globally integrated economy than was either the United Kingdom or the United States when they became superpowers. In 1870, exports accounted for only 12 percent of the United Kingdom's output. In 1975, exports accounted for a mere 7 percent of the US economy. In 2008, 35 percent of China's economic output was exported. We have seen economist Richard Baldwin calculate that the Chinese content of its own processing exports is less than 20 percent—that is, four-fifths of the parts China exports in final products are sourced from abroad. Thus, the same level of trade implies a far higher level of global integration than it did in the past.[5]

A further sign of China's integration is the fact that 50 percent of the country's exports were produced by foreign-controlled enterprises in 2008. That's not to mention China's own investments overseas. The country has over $3 trillion in foreign reserves alone, most held in securities (and a good chunk in the United States and Europe).[6]

This all suggests that China will remain a fair-dealing member of the World Trade Organization and the International Monetary Fund out of self-interest (if an active participant in WTO-mediated trade disputes—in 2009 half of the disputes filed involved China on one side or the other). And the WTO has already shown itself to be a powerful mechanism for controlling the bullying instincts of the top nation—the United States has been subject to complaints in eighty-eight WTO disputes, thirty-three violations were established, and the United States has complied or is in the process of complying in twenty-six cases.[7]

∘ ∘ ∘

BUT WHAT ABOUT THE FACT that economic dominance will allow a nondemocratic country to expand its military reach? It is less than a quarter-century since the Chinese government turned soldiers and tanks on unarmed citizens in the heart of its capital, and only fifty years since the Communist Party's so-called Great Leap Forward killed tens of millions. Dissidents are still regularly imprisoned or disappear. And only in the past few years has China helped block international responses to deal with the thuggish regimes of Syria's Bashar al-Assad and Sudan's Omar al-Bashir, while propping up North Korea's famine-ridden kleptocracy. China is the world's sixth-largest arms exporter overall and accounts for 25 percent of the sub-Saharan arms market outside of South Africa. Weapons from China regularly pop up in war zones from the Democratic Republic of Congo to the Ivory Coast, Sudan, and Somalia, and the country has not been shy about using its seat on the UN Security Council to stymie UN arms investigations. All of this suggests the potential for an autocratic economic powerhouse to use its growing financial muscle to fund military adventures on a grand scale.[8]

Certainly, given that democracies so rarely go to war and that the considerable majority of the world's population already lives under a democratic regime, it would be a huge step for both global security and China's domestic human rights were the country to become a stable democracy.

Still, the correlation between democracy and a pacific external stance is less than perfect—as the histories of the United States and China themselves demonstrate. The short 1979 Sino-Vietnam War was China's last international armed conflict—and it didn't even end with a border change. Compare that to the long list of American interventions prior to the end of World War I— it hardly suggests that young democratic superpowers are particularly peaceful. In the twenty years prior to 1918, the United States had occupied Cuba, the Philippines, Haiti, Nicaragua, the Dominican Republic, the Panama Canal Zone, and Puerto Rico, and it had sent troops to fight in Mexico, Western Europe, and Russia. In fact, just over the past thirty years the list of unpleasant groups provided with arms and cash by a democratic America is a long one. Take just two examples: the Taliban in Afghanistan and Saddam Hussein's regime in Iraq. The United States helped arm both before it went to war with them.

So the hopes for a comparatively benign Chinese global military policy had better rest on more than the development of domestic liberties—even were such liberties to become firmly entrenched. Luckily they do. In fact, such hopes rely on the fact that China is far more enmeshed in the international system than any previous superpower, including the United States, as well as on this being a world where military dominance isn't what it used to be.

The nature of global power itself has changed dramatically over the past two centuries, from being based in geographical domination to being largely based not in physical goods—let alone land—but in finance, technologies, and services. Just as the United States advanced over the United Kingdom by needing only access to markets rather than a sovereign empire to dominate the world economy, in a new, more pacific age, China will not need the kind of military strength enjoyed by the United States for the last fifty years to remain preeminent. And that's in large part thanks to the global economic and political institutions that the United States itself set up over the past sixty years.

At the same time as the importance to global power of geographical occupation has declined, wars have become increasingly difficult to win. A century ago, the United Kingdom's "two-navy" strategy (having a fleet as large as the next two major powers combined) was part of a successful effort to control one-quarter of the world's land area. Only seventy-odd years ago, the world's most powerful alliance took on two major economic powers and crushed them in six years. But World War II was almost the end of the era when states could invade and occupy another country and then leave as an ally.

It worked to some extent in Cambodia after Vietnam's invasion, and with Tanzania's intervention in Uganda, but such cases are rare. In fact, the number of real attempts by one country to occupy another militarily for any length of time has dramatically shrunk—making Iraq's invasion of Kuwait and America's more recent adventures in Iraq and Afghanistan, for example, look anachronistic. The far more fashionable way to use military force or supplies in the recent past has been the limited support of one side or another in an ongoing civil war. Related to this, a large military is by no means a cure-all for national security concerns:

US global military dominance has hardly led to the solution of the Arab-Israeli disputes, or eased tensions between North and South Korea, or bolstered Pakistani stability, despite considerable and obvious American interests in such settlements.[9]

As well as the greater challenge of winning a war in a world where opponents don't appear willing to give up after the tanks have rolled through their capital city, the changing global nature of economic engagement makes war between major trading partners in particular a far less sustainable endeavor. When trade was a smaller part of the global economy and almost exclusively involved commodities and finished goods, war had a comparatively minor impact on output. Pretty much every country produced most of what it needed to make the goods it consumed and exported. When this was not the case, it was a major factor in conflict. The closest the United Kingdom came to defeat in both world wars was because it needed imported raw materials and agricultural products to feed its people and factories, and for a time German submarines were sinking enough shipping to endanger that supply. Likewise, Germany needed oil, which was why its alliance with oil-producing Romania was so important to its military strategy in the Second World War. But today, as we have seen, trade has grown overall, and trade in parts is a far more important component of global goods exchange. If China declared global war, its economy would quickly grind to a halt because it doesn't make the components its factories need to build final products.

Regardless, there is far more to global *military* power than brute economic output statistics. In 1870, when Britain was undoubtedly top nation, it accounted for 9 percent of global output (although the empire as a whole produced far more). The US economy was already almost the same size. China's share accounted for almost the same as both combined—at 17 percent of global output.[10] But 1870 was only ten years after a treaty ending a war between China and Britain that had humiliated the larger economy—China was forced to open its borders to foreign goods, including opium from India.

Perhaps this is one reason why, as recently as 2010, Harvard international relations professor Joseph Nye approvingly cited the National Intelligence Council's prediction that the United States, while slipping, would remain the most significant global power in 2025.[11] Similarly, Carla Hills and Dennis Blair concluded in a report for the Council on Foreign Relations that "the military balance today and for the foreseeable future strongly favors the United States and its allies."[12]

Certainly, China's military strength is rising, but no analyst would suggest that the country has anywhere near the ability to project military power onto the global stage today. The country currently has but one aircraft carrier, which has no aircraft based on it. An aircraft carrier that has no aircraft to carry must have some serious existential issues. As if that weren't bad enough, it's a thirdhand boat—a hand-me-down from the Soviet Union to Ukraine that China picked up at a yard sale in 1998. Meanwhile, the United States has twenty carriers—all of which come with actual planes. Overall, China's military expenditure may have grown eightfold from 1989 to 2009, but it is still dwarfed by the United States. China accounts for only around 8 percent of global military expenditure compared to 41 percent for America, according to the Stockholm Peace Research Institute.[13]

Additionally, China's geostrategic position is considerably less secure than is that of the United States. The United States formally guarantees the security of more than fifty countries— that's a lot of allies. Compare the Middle Kingdom, surrounded by fourteen countries, many of which are antagonistic. And while a few thousand people have signed Texas independence petitions, China faces significant challenges from internal regional independence groups, from Tibet through East Turkestan, that get support from abroad.[14] "The American military is deployed all around China's periphery," note Andrew Nathan and Andrew Scobell in a recent *Foreign Affairs* article. "Washington continues to frustrate Beijing's efforts to gain control over Taiwan [and] the United States constantly pressures China over its economic policies and maintains a host of government and private programs that seek to influence Chinese civil society and politics." (For China, this must all evoke distant memories of the Opium Wars.)[15]

Perhaps China's greater enmeshment in the global economy and its comparatively exposed geostrategic position are associated with its lower prioritization of military dominance. Perhaps the United States has cowed China into focusing on its economic dominance. Or perhaps China has learned from the recent US experience that military dominance may not be worth the effort or expense. Whatever the reason, the Chinese people appear to have considerably more pacific and cosmopolitan attitudes than even Americans of today in some cases. It is true that World Values Survey evidence suggests that Chinese say they trust people of different nationalities less than do Americans. But 84 percent of Chinese people agree, when asked, that they see themselves as world citizens, compared to 69 percent of Americans. Asked who should decide policies about international peacekeeping, 64 percent of Chinese pick the UN over national governments or regional organizations, compared to 53 percent in the United States. (Relative support for the UN does switch when it comes to deciding policies toward human rights.) The Middle Kingdom does not appear to be a country filled with either isolationists or militarists. And it is a country that appears to have no pretensions to global military dominance—at least not anytime soon.

o   o   o

THERE IS A LOT MORE to life than global economic and military leadership, of course, but being biggest and among the richest hasn't helped the United States stake a global lead on measures of the broader quality of life either.

The website Ranking America is a treasure trove of statistics on America's standing in the world. We have seen that it has the largest GDP at market rates and the greatest military expenditure by any measure. And America has the largest whey supply in the world, with more than half of global production. The laws of chemistry dictate that the country must therefore also lead the world in curds production, but much of that probably gets thrown out. At the same time, the United States was only second in global alfalfa exports in 2010, ranking behind Spain. It ranks a measly forty-sixth in sheep stocks, with a flock a little over 5.5 million strong. It is the twenty-fourth most free of corruption, according to Transparency International. It ranks fifty-sixth in terms of the equality of women's and men's pay. The United States ranks second *highest* out of the Organization for Economic Cooperation and Development (OECD) club of rich countries in the proportion of children in poverty, and only forty-seventh worldwide in infant survival. The proportion of kids who die before the age of one in the United States—around six in every one thousand—is three times the level in Monaco. Americans face the fifth-longest average commuting time of all OECD countries. And it is only eleventh in happiness, according to the Earth Institute. (Canada is fifth, and the Nordics and the Netherlands take the top spots.)[16]

Or take a list of the rich countries Australia, Austria, Canada, Denmark, Finland, France, Germany, the Netherlands, Norway, Singapore, Sweden, Switzerland, the United Kingdom, and the United States. The United States is at the bottom of that list in life expectancy, as well as the only country without universal health care, according to the OECD.[17] The United States is at the tail end of the list when it comes to its citizens' belief in basic scientific truths like evolution, and it scores lowest out of all these countries on international tests of student mathematics performance.[18]

So, if you were choosing where to be born, which country would you pick? Maybe Monaco, if you really wanted to minimize your chance of dying as a child — or maximize your chance of spending time around super-yachts. Maybe Norway or Sweden, if you cared about equality of opportunity at high levels of income, good public health care, strong education systems, an understated monarchy, and close access to fjords. Maybe the United States, if what concerned you most was a high standard of living across a whole range of measures in a large, geographically fascinating country that is the world's most militarily powerful. Given the country's dominance in curds and whey production, you also might choose the United States if you were a member of the Muffet family, sitting on your tuffet and feeling peckish. There are many plausible answers, then, to which is the world's *best* country. The United States (or Germany, or the United Kingdom) would be the answer on some measures and emphatically wouldn't be on others. In no way does the top military and economic spot translate as top-of-everything dominance.

On the bright side for those who worry about losing out to China in gross output, the United States still considerably outperforms that country on almost every conceivable quality-of-life indicator, including happiness (where China is in seventieth place worldwide). The average American lives five years longer than the average Chinese person, while mortality rates for children under the age of five are less than half of the Chinese levels. And for all that you may not think much of the abilities of Congress and the president when it comes to managing the US economy—or even managing their way out of a paper bag—they remain the voters' to throw out. The same cannot yet be said of the leadership of the Communist Party of China.

Again, even if the United States and China have equal GDP, a lot more Chinese people have to share the same domestic product. That's why, using the World Bank's statistics, the average person in China lives on an income that can buy only 16 percent of the goods and services of the average person in the United States.[19] Even the rosiest projections for Chinese growth suggest that it will take decades for the income gap with the United States to close. If you're an American feeling down about losing top economy status, go take a holiday in Guizhou. That's a poor province in the west of China where incomes are about one-fortieth as high as the US average at market exchange rates (the rates you get at the foreign currency desk). You'll feel a lot better.[20]

All of this applies to Europe as well. Countries that have long since demonstrated to the United States that being at the top of one league table doesn't guarantee being at the top of the lot should have no fear of being overtaken by China in terms of quality of life anytime soon. And even if that day should come, it will almost certainly be because of Chinese improvement, not European decline.

○ ○ ○

IF YOU ARE STILL WORRIED by China's rise, compare the country to the Soviet Union, the last threatening superpower. A system whose leadership had become committed to "socialism in one country" prior to world revolution was far less integrated with the global economy than China has been for a long time. For all of China's lip service to a similar communist belief system, policy practitioners in today's China have largely abandoned that ideology, and the country has no pretensions to fomenting global revolution. Treating China like a worthy successor to the Soviet Union as an American foe to be faced with staunch and massive military, diplomatic, and economic containment would be an incredibly counterproductive and costly mistake.

The West should engage China and try to deepen its ties with a global trading and financial system that can help ensure the country remains a positive force for global peace and prosperity. The more China embraces its role as an economic heavyweight on an integrated planet, the better it'll be for the rest of the world (and perhaps in particular the United States) in terms of national security and economic opportunity. Even for Americans who fear the inevitable rise of China, then, the best advice may come from Chinese philosopher Sun Tzu, as reinterpreted by the US realist thinker Michael Corleone in *The Godfather:* keep your friends close and your enemies closer.

Meanwhile, on the home front, rather than wringing our hands over the irrelevance of America's relative global economic weight, we should remember the wisdom of the founding fathers and focus instead on preserving and extending life, liberty, and the pursuit of happiness. If the good news is that losing the top GDP spot doesn't matter in terms of quality of life or security, the even better news is that a wealthier, healthier, and happier world can help the United States improve its broader quality of life even more. As the planet rids itself of diseases from smallpox to rinderpest to polio, Americans are permanently protected from their threat. As development and integration reduce the threat of war, the need for a large military declines. As other economies expand, the opportunities to trade with and invest or work in them increase as well. That is the subject of the next chapter.

CHAPTER FOUR

The Rise of the Rest Is Good for the West

IN JANUARY 2012, President Barack Obama climbed to the podium to deliver the last State of the Union address of his first term. With the recovery looking fragile and unemployment still above 8 percent, he had to sell America on his economic policies in advance of the election. "Let's remember how we got here," he noted. "Long before the recession, jobs and manufacturing began leaving our shores." The good news? "Right now, it's getting more expensive to do business in places like China. Meanwhile, America is more productive." So his message to business leaders was simple: "Ask yourselves what you can do to bring jobs back to your country." He told the story of Jackie Bray, a single mother from North Carolina who was laid off from her job as a mechanic. But then Siemens opened a gas turbine factory in Charlotte. The company paid Jackie's tuition for laser and robotics training and then hired her to help operate its plant. But the government would do its part too, said Obama; not least, it would enact trade policies to protect workers. "Over a thousand Americans are working today because we stopped a surge in Chinese tires," he noted.

There was a lot that was wrongheaded in those State of the Union remarks—in particular, the implication that one new manufacturing job in China implies one lost in the United States, and the idea that trade wars like the one over tires protect US jobs. The president also ignored the fact that the reason it is getting more expensive to do business in China is that wages have gone up—thanks to that country's export-led growth.

But Mr. Obama's example of a business doing the *right* thing is also interesting. Siemens is a German company. Presumably the president thought it was good that a Western company was investing in manufacturing jobs overseas, in this case at least. And we'll see that Germany as a whole has done far better than the United States at retraining manufacturing workers and keeping them employed. In Charlotte, while Washington was too busy ensuring that other Americans lost their jobs through counter-productive trade spats, Siemens was paying the tuition of a job-less person so she could stay in the workforce (the kind of policy that the German government supports).

The president's remarks evoke a popular school of thought among those scarred by courses in international relations that take the global economy as a zero-sum game. That school sees every call center opening in Bangalore as lost jobs in Birmingham or Binghamton, every shirt made in Mauritius as one less made in Mobile, every sugarcane grown in Brazil as a stake through the heart of a Florida cane farmer.

But a bigger, richer, more homogeneous global economy offers huge opportunities to the West. America's exports to fast-growing developing economies are already booming, investment flowing in both directions will strengthen the global economy, and stronger innovation systems in developing countries will mean greater technological progress worldwide. All this is good for everyone. And a convergence in global values will ensure that the international movement of goods, people, and finance becomes ever more straightforward and rewarding. The rise of the Rest is the greatest news for the West since the fall of the Berlin Wall—quite possibly even better news than that. Taken altogether, these forces should also help preserve a new era of comparative global peace and broader well-being.

o   o   o

WHEN IT COMES TO new markets for Western products, US and European companies should look forward to a bonanza rising in the East. According to the Asian Development Bank, if strong growth in the region continues, Asia will have a 51 percent share of the global economy, almost double its current share, compared to 18 percent for Europe and 15 percent for North America in 2050. Even if Asia gets stuck in a "middle-income trap," suffering slower growth because its institutions of government aren't up to the challenge of underpinning the complex relations of an advanced economy, it will still have a 32 percent share of global GDP, compared to 26 percent for Europe and 23 percent for North America. Asia's share of global GDP will increase not because the West will shrink, but because the East will grow faster. And that means more money—and markets—for everyone.[1]

Brookings economist Homi Kharas estimates that the global "middle class" (which he defines as those living on between $10 and $100 a day) will expand from 1.8 billion people in 2009 to

4.9 billion people in 2030. These are the people rich enough to own a car and spend money on personal products and services. Today about half of the world's $10-plus-per-day middle class lives in developing countries. By 2030, two-thirds will live in the Asia-Pacific region alone, compared to 21 percent who will live in North America and Europe. The Middle East and Africa will have as many middle-class residents as North America.[2]

All of those middle-class people will be able to splurge on a meal out once in a while. And that's why the fast-food chain KFC is emblematic of a number of the changes going on in the global economy. It is a Western company finding its greatest investment opportunities in the developing world. Those developing-country consumers are buying KFC's product in part for its status association with the United States. Less positively, the product they are buying is exactly the kind of food that's driving a global obesity epidemic—speeding a worldwide convergence toward diseases of the rich.

Yum! Brands, which owns KFC along with Pizza Hut and Taco Bell, operates 37,000 restaurants in 120 countries. While it is closing stores in the United States and losing market share, KFC frontman Colonel Sanders has proven to be far more popular overseas than a number of other US military figures of late. China alone was home to 3,701 KFCs in 2011—about three-quarters the number in the United States—and by 2014, Africa will have about 1,200 KFCs, selling $2 billion worth of breasts, legs, and sides, the great majority deep-fried.[3]

Similarly, America still apparently leads the world in selling the overpriced latte lifestyle. Starbucks will have over 1,500 stores in more than 70 cities in China by 2015—making the country Starbucks's second-largest market after the United States itself. In the last quarter of 2011, operating margins on those stores neared

35 percent—the highest of any region in which the company operates, and compared to a meager 22 percent for US stores. And India is next—Starbucks entered into a joint venture with a local firm in mid-2012, and the first store opened that year.[4]

Beer provides another global opportunity for Western brands from Guinness to Schlitz. In 1980 beer consumption in China was minimal. Today the country consumes more than 40 billion liters. In 1961, Brazil drank 630 million liters of beer, and in 2005 that number was 7.5 billion liters. Breweries are often some of the first foreign investors to show up in even the most fragile of states. Just in 2011–2012, Heineken bid on two state-owned breweries in Ethiopia for $163 million; the first-ever IPO on Rwanda's stock exchange involved the local brewery raising funds from foreign investors; and SAB Miller put in an additional $15 million on top of a 2009 $37 million investment in its operation in Juba, South Sudan.[5]

Meanwhile, other Western firms are benefiting from the health problems created by all of those crispy wings and triple caramel mochachinos and pints. It might be seen as odd given the chronic cost-ineffectiveness of the US medical system compared to other countries in the OECD, but China is looking to America, which has the world's largest private health system, to provide advice and investment in its own growing private health sector. Rule changes in China in early 2012 allowed for foreign companies to fully own hospitals, and US firms, including Concord Medical Services Holdings, plan to move into a market that may be worth $500 billion by 2015.[6]

And this story of growing opportunities in a richer Rest spreads far beyond the Asian tigers. Africa attracted a record share of foreign direct investment in 2011—5.5 percent of the global total, considerably larger than its share of global market GDP. South

Africa, Nigeria, and Angola between them are forecast to attract more than $40 billion in foreign direct investment from 2012 to 2017, reports Ernst and Young. Bob Geldof, the Boomtown Rat previously best known for hating Mondays and fighting African famine, raised $200 million for an African private equity fund in 2012. Helios, another London-based group, closed a $900 million Africa fund in 2011.[7]

○ ○ ○

OF COURSE, SKEPTICS SUGGEST that US and European investment overseas comes at the cost of Western workers, who lose out when firms move their factories from Baltimore to Mumbai. But even economists concerned about the impact of increased trade competition on American workers, like Harvard's Avraham Ebenstein, argue that offshoring plays a minor role—if any role at all—in overall US wage and employment trends.[8] Greg Wright of the University of Essex estimates that US offshoring may have been responsible for a 1.6 percent decline in manufacturing jobs over the period 1997 to 2007, but the impact on long-term productivity may actually increase employment (which may also be better paid). The idea is that firms save money by offshoring, which, by allowing them to sell more for less, increases both their own revenues and the revenues of those that purchase the goods they sell. As a result, they can hire more people, or their shareholders have more money to buy goods and services from other Americans.[9]

Similarly, Rujuan Liu and Daniel Trefler's analysis for the National Bureau of Economic Research suggests that US workers in occupations exposed to outsourcing—which were also industries that benefited from the ability to "inshore" work from abroad—

were slightly *less* likely to be unemployed and earned 1.5 percent more thanks to the growth of their industry from 1996 to 2005. And an increasing amount of investment abroad is in nontraded sectors like KFC restaurants and local hospitals, which present limited potential for any trade-off at all between jobs here and jobs there.[10] Such investments are all on the upside for residents of the United States.

Meanwhile, a lot of money is flowing the other way—from developing countries to invest in the United States and Europe. Already, fifty-six out of the *Financial Times'* list of the world's five hundred largest companies in 2012 were in Brazil, India, China, or Russia, and those companies had a combined valuation of $3.3 trillion. Many of these companies are expanding overseas.[11]

Chinese investment in the European Union topped $10 billion in 2011, and China's investment in the United States climbed from $3 billion in 2011 to $8 billion in just the first three quarters of 2012. Notably, AMC movie theaters are now owned by the Chinese firm Dalian Wanda. By 2020, forecasts by the New York–based Rhodium Group suggest that the stock of Chinese investment in the United States could reach $200 billion and employ 400,000 Americans. As an example, Lenovo announced in 2012 that it would start making personal computers in the United States—which IBM's hardware arm, purchased by Lenovo a few years ago, stopped doing a couple of decades ago.[12]

Britain, meanwhile, is a major beneficiary of investment from India, its former colony. Tata is a conglomerate controlled by Lakshmi Mittal, the Indian-born entrepreneur who is now Britain's richest resident. Tata UK was the country's largest manufacturer in 2011, employing 40,000 people. The company owns most of what is left of the British steel industry, as well as Jaguar

Land Rover—the rump of Britain's domestic car manufacturing base. Tata also controls Tetley, which, as the company that invented the tea bag, is as significant a British national institution as the horse guards or deep-fried Mars bars. In making these acquisitions, Tata was buying a brand name as well as specialist techniques. But it also invested considerable sums in UK firms (some would argue that it overpaid for them) and preserved British jobs in the process.

These examples are not confined to China in the United States and India in the United Kingdom. Mexico's Cemex is now the largest US producer of cement, while the country's Grupo Bimbo bought out US baker Sara Lee in a near-billion-dollar deal in 2010.[13]

The wealthier parts of the developing world are also playing a growing role in helping the poorer parts catch up. About 14 percent of China's outward investment, for example, flows to Africa, where it goes to a range of sectors, including about 22 percent to manufacturing and 29 percent to mining.[14] All of this activity further expands markets and opportunities for Western firms in the region.

o o o

TURNING TO TRADE, despite the legitimate concerns that Western imports from the developing world are responsible for declining employment, or at least the displacement of manufacturing jobs, at home, their overall impact remains strongly positive. The share of total US spending on Chinese goods rose from $1 out of every $170 in 1991 to $1 out of every $22 in 2007. Why? One big reason is that Chinese imports are cheaper than products produced in the United States. During the period 1999 to 2003 alone, rising Chinese imports reduced the price of nondurable goods (food, cosmetics, office supplies) in the United States by 2.8 percent. Poorer people buy more nondurable goods than rich people as a proportion of their overall expenditure, so Chinese imports had a particularly beneficial impact on people at the bottom of America's income distribution. Over the period 1994 to 2005, prices for goods purchased by the poorest tenth of the population increased six percentage points less than prices for the richest 10 percent of Americans because of growing trade with China.[15]

But we considerably underestimate the benefits of trade if we look only at the price of goods. A huge advantage of trade is to increase *choices* among goods. With global trade, you can choose between Hershey's Kisses and Belgian truffles, Bud Light and Amstel Light. One estimate is that this extra choice was worth about $260 billion to US consumers—or 3 percent of US GDP—in 2001.[16]

And developing countries in particular are exporting more and more different types of goods to the United States, expanding the choices of US consumers. China, for example, exported only 510 types of goods to the United States in 1972. By 2001 that had climbed to 10,199 types of goods. In that year, Chinese exporters competed in nearly two-thirds of all US import markets by type of goods. It ranked fourth out of countries worldwide in terms of the number of different goods it sent to the United States, behind only Canada, the United Kingdom, and Germany. Mexico, Taiwan, and South Korea also made it into the top ten.

Put these two factors together, lower prices and more choice, and they suggest that imports from developing countries have been a considerable boon for average Americans—and perhaps especially for the poorest Americans. Cheaper goods have also made the US economy more efficient—it can produce more goods at a lower price thanks to lower input costs—and that is good for overall employment.

Some of those imports did, however, replace goods formerly made in American factories by American workers. As a result, according to MIT's David Autor and his colleagues, Chinese exports were responsible for manufacturing job losses equal to around eight out of every one thousand people of working age in the United States between 1990 and 2007—as many as 1.5 million jobs.[17] An analysis for the National Bureau of Economic Research also suggests that increased competition from enterprises in the developing world has significantly dampened American manufacturing wages.[18]

But the good news for those concerned about manufacturing employment is that it climbed back from its nadir of 11,458,000 in January 2010 to 11,942,000 in September 2012. One reason noted by President Obama in his 2012 State of the Union address was that Chinese wages are rising. The Boston Consulting Group notes that the labor cost advantage between China and the poorer US states will fall from 55 percent in 2011 to 39 percent by 2015, suggesting that more US manufacturing jobs may be coming.[19] Later in the book we will also see that had the United States followed the German model of greater support for retraining and relocating workers, the dip in manufacturing employment need not have been so steep.

And the more important point is that while some firms lost jobs in competition to China, other firms benefited from cheaper imports and were able to grow—in other words, fewer Chinese imports might have *lowered* overall employment in the United States. Take the tariffs that President Obama slapped on Chinese tire imports, which he celebrated in his 2012 State of the

Union. Gary Hufbauer of the Peterson Institute suggests that each job in the tire industry saved by the tariffs cost Americans at least $900,000 in more expensive tires. That left less money to spend on other goods, weakening demand for a range of American products. The net impact of the tariff was 2,500 lost American jobs.[20]

Again, we've seen that with the growing importance of the trade in parts, a lot of what China exports is made up of components originally manufactured elsewhere, including in the West. More than 90 percent of the value of China's high-tech exports, for instance, is produced by foreign-controlled firms—what Chinese workers are adding is assembly and low-tech components.

Take the iPhone and iPad. Sure, they are imported from China, but most of the stuff in them doesn't come from there. A new iPhone costs in the region of $179 wholesale. The American-made parts inside are worth $10.75—that's considerably more than the $6.50 that Chinese labor adds to the final cost. Japanese, Korean, and German components account for another $114. US companies, including Apple, have done very well designing products that are built overseas and managing global production chains and marketing. This kind of industrial activity is much more high-value than being stuck in commodity manufacturing, and it is one more reason why the United States benefits from growing Chinese exports.[21]

Still, it is easier to persuade Western workers that exporting their goods to the developing world is a great thing. And there is a lot more of that going on as well. In the year 2000, the developing world imported about one-third of global exports. The developed world accounted for the other two-thirds. In 2012, according to *The Economist*, the developing world imported more than half of the world's exports. China will import more than the United States by 2014. And almost three-fifths of American exports were heading to emerging markets by 2012, more than double the proportion in 1990.[22]

Even Africa is a growing market for Western goods. The British-Dutch firm Unilever—which makes consumer goods from Dove soap to Knorr soups—already has a $4 billion market in Africa and hopes to double it by 2017. Nigeria is the third-largest global consumer of iron-rich Guinness beer, much to the benefit of the drinks multinational Diageo, a company that already makes 14 percent of its sales in Africa. Nestlé, meanwhile, had African sales totaling $3.6 billion in 2010.[23]

At the other end of the scale, a particular area of trade where the West seems to have a continuing comparative advantage is the sale of ridiculously overpriced fripperies, from sixty-year-old single malt whiskey to impossible-to-wear designer clothes. Think, for example, of the Hermes Matte Crocodile Birkin Bag at $120,000, or the Wagyu Meat Pie from the Fence Gate Inn in the United Kingdom—six pounds of Kobe beef, matsutake mushrooms, truffles, two bottles of Chateau Mouton Rothschild, and edible gold leaf, for $16,000.

What is the market for such blindingly conspicuous consumption? High-net-worth individuals, also known as the obscenely rich. And as the rest of the world gets better off, the number of such individuals grows. According to "The Wealth Report 2012" from Knight Frank and Citi Private Bank, the number of people worth more than $100 million a year increased 29 percent from 2006 to 2011. That was hardly the easiest time to make money in the West—and indeed, the centamillionaire growth rate in North America over the same period was a paltry, Occupy Wall Street–pleasing 7 percent. Western Europe actually had fewer obscenely rich in 2011 than it did in 2006.[24] But the number of high-net-worth individuals tripled over the same five-year period in South and Central Asia and went up 80 percent in Southeast Asia. Add up Asia, Africa, Eastern Europe, and Latin America and the number of centamillionaires in 2011 came to around 32,000—just over half of the world total.

That's one reason why the Knight Frank survey suggests that China's luxury goods market is growing at 35 percent a year, with Prada and Gucci opening stores "in cities mostly unknown outside China." British luxury car maker Bentley sold 1,839 cars in China in 2011, double the number from a year before. And the Asia-Pacific region as a whole accounted for 27 percent of global luxury spending that year, up from 16 percent in 2006.

More generally, as George Mason University's Tyler Cowen has argued, "the leading categories of American exports today—civilian aircraft, semiconductors, cars, pharmaceuticals, machinery and equipment, automobile accessories, and entertainment—are going to be in the sweet spot of growing demand in what we now call the developing world."[25]

Looking at pharmaceuticals in particular, the IMS Institute for Healthcare Economics estimates that global spending on medicines will reach $1.1 trillion in 2015, up from $600 billion in 2005. That growth will be driven by developing markets. Seventeen high-growth emerging markets, led by China, will account for 28 percent of total spending by 2015, up from 12 percent in 2005. And the big driver in developing markets will be diseases of the rich. For example, global spending on diabetes will increase by 4 to 7 percent from 2011 to 2016, driven by rapid growth in type 2 diabetes and treatment rates, especially in countries such as China, India, Mexico, and Brazil. What is bad news for continued rapid progress in quality of life in middle-income countries is great news for Merck and other producers of diabetes drugs.[26]

When it comes to automobiles, the rest of the world has been an important part of the revival of the US industry. According to Brookings's Kharas, in 2000 the United States accounted for 37 percent of global car purchases, compared to 1 percent for China. By 2009, China was the world's largest auto market, buying three million more vehicles in that year than US consumers. GM sold one car in China for each ten in the United States in 2004, but by 2009 that ratio was approaching one-to-one.[27]

And in the entertainment industry, foreign sales were the one reason why Hollywood's 2011 *Battleship*, which performed domestically like *Titanic* the boat rather than *Titanic* the movie, didn't completely sink its producers. Nearly four-fifths of its $303 million box office came from testosterone-addled teens and fellow travelers outside of the United States. Even films that are successful in malls across America make more abroad—the last Harry Potter movie made more than twice as much in the rest of the world as in the United States. In total, international revenue accounted for 69 percent of Hollywood's box-office receipts in 2011, with growth driven by emerging markets. China alone saw the number of movie theaters double from 2007 to 2011; the country is projected to have 16,500 screens by 2015.[28]

And entertainment is only one part of a growing Western export market in services to the rest of the world. The travel and passenger fares export sector is worth $722 billion a year to the US economy, according to the US Bureau of Economic Analysis, and the nouveau riche of Asia account for an ever-larger percentage of that revenue. Not least, Chinese tourists now outspend the Brits and the French in the United States—and spend twice as much as Italians and Japanese.[29]

Looking at other service sectors, the United States has fifty-three universities in the top one hundred worldwide, as ranked by Shanghai University.[30] That allows America to attract some of the world's best students—as well as some of the world's richest ones. There are 723,000 foreign students studying in the country. The University of Washington (sixteenth in the Shanghai University rankings) charges the 18 percent of its students who enroll from overseas around $28,000 a year—three times the in-state tuition rate. And as the Rest has grown richer, the number of developing-country undergraduates studying in US universities has expanded. The number of Chinese undergraduates in the United States alone rose by 57,000 in the five years prior to 2012—an almost sixfold increase. International students at US colleges contribute $21 billion to the economy, according to the Institute of International Education.[31] That alone accounts for around one-seventh of our entire services trade surplus.[32]

Of course, we'll see that it is also true that there are increasing opportunities for bright young Europeans and Americans to study in the developing world, which might dent the service trade surplus. The US share of the top five hundred universities has been falling, with almost every American entry that drops out being replaced by a Chinese school—twenty-three Chinese universities were included in 2011, up from only nine in 2003. There is no evidence, however, that this reflects a declining quality of education in the United States—and in a rapidly expanding global market for tertiary education, some additional competition will pose little threat to US services exports growth.

o o o

STILL, WHAT IF THE TREND to higher-quality education in China and elsewhere translates into growing technological muscle, turning Silicon Valley into an innovation backwater compared to Bangalore or Shanghai? There is already a considerable fear that the United States is losing technological leadership. Former energy secretary Stephen Chu warned as early as 2010 that China might be the world leader in innovation on some measures by 2011. The consulting firm KPMG surveyed 650 business executives in 2012, and 30 percent of respondents suggested that China would be the biggest "global hotspot" for innovation over the next four years, compared to 29 percent who said it would be the United States. And India beat out Japan for third place.[33]

It is true that, in 2006, China was producing twice the number of science and engineering graduates as the United States, and also that, in just six years from 2002 to 2008, the US lead in peer-reviewed scientific article publication had been cut by more than half, from a sixfold advantage to only two and a half times.[34] By 2004, China had become the fifth-largest producer of academic scientific publications registered in the SCI Web of Science — behind the United Kingdom, Germany, Japan, and the United States.[35]

Meanwhile, outside of universities, the number of multinational enterprise research and development centers in China rose to 1,100 by the end of 2008, with another 780 in India. And the World Intellectual Property Organization reports that filings under the Patent Cooperation Treaty from China tripled from 2006 to 2010, from under 4,000 to over 12,000.[36]

This may all be translating into more innovative business. Every year *Forbes* magazine comes up with a list of the world's most innovative publicly listed companies, using a measure of the stock price of a firm above the value of its existing business. This, they say, is based on market expectations of future innovative results (new products, services, and markets). One might well argue with the selection procedure. But it's at least some indication of growth potential based on new approaches to making money.[37]

The global top four most innovative companies in 2012 were based in the United States—customer relations management firm Salesforce.com, Alexion Pharmaceuticals (which recently published positive results from a drug trial for treating a life-threatening neurological disorder), online retailer Amazon.com, and Linux developer Red Hat. But number five was Baidu—a Chinese web services company. In fact, China alone occupied seven spots out of the top one hundred, with India occupying another five. It is worth comparing those numbers with Germany's (six in the top one hundred) and the United Kingdom's (just four). The Asian giants are punching their weight on this measure of innovation at least.

So a number of measures suggest that the Rest is becoming more innovative. But it is still a long way behind the West. In 2012, China earned $1 billion in royalty and license payments from overseas—this for intellectual property that the country had created that was being exploited by firms elsewhere. It paid $18 billion in royalty and license payments to foreign firms, for a total deficit of $17 billion. Compare that to the United States, which ran an $82 billion *surplus*.[38]

Regardless, it is particularly ridiculous to view greater innovation and creativity in the Rest as a *threat* to the West. The idea that inventing new things in particular is a zero-sum game is a madness reminiscent of the apocryphal story regarding the US patent officer declaring in 1900 that everything that could be invented had been invented. There is no finite number of things to innovate, so one more innovation overseas doesn't somehow translate into fewer jobs or profits at home. Indeed, the reverse is true: we all benefit from more global innovation. Is the United Kingdom worse off because the measles vaccine was developed in the United States? Or is the United States worse off because writing was invented in the Fertile Crescent?

A richer and more educated global population will just increase humanity's stock of knowledge, products, and techniques and produce more people like Kumar Patel (Indian-born inventor of the carbon dioxide laser), Rangaswamy Srinivasan (Indian-born inventor of LASIK eye surgery), Lázló Bíró (Hungarian-born inventor of the ballpoint in Argentina), and Luis Miramontes (Mexican co-inventor of the oral contraceptive)—not to mention more business leaders such as mobile phone CEO Mo Ibrahim (Sudan), moral forces like Desmond Tutu (South Africa), musical talents like Youssou N'Dour (Senegal), sports legends like Pelé (Brazil), and literary giants like Salman Rushdie (India).

And in fact, a lot of these talented people (including Kumar Patel and Rangaswamy Srinivasan) make their way to the United States. A study for the Partnership for a New American Economy found that 76 percent of patents awarded to the top ten patent-producing US universities in 2011 involved at least one foreign-born inventor. The thousand-plus patents included inventors from eighty-eight different countries. For example, the Indian who helped develop the most efficient desalinization technology currently available was in America when he did it— based at the University of California at Los Angeles.[39]

Looking at recent innovations developed in India itself, we see that the Tata Nano, a no-frills Indian car that cost only $2,000, hardly took off (although some early versions did take flight, all too literally), but other innovations are doing better. The country's pharmaceutical industry has driven down the cost of vaccine production and developed treatments for HIV/AIDS that combine multiple drugs in a single pill, considerably simplifying life for those on antiretrovirals. Or look at Shree Cement, which has developed the world's most water-efficient cement manufacturing system by substituting air cooling for water cooling. And Western companies are investing in these innovative Indian companies: Siemens's Mumbai-based subsidiary was working on forty-two products in 2010 for the Indian market, including solar-powered X-ray machines and steam turbines. These cheaper, simpler, and more robust products developed for markets in developing countries may end up expanding markets in the West—cheap electrocardiogram machines developed for Indian hospitals, for instance, are now sold to rural doctors in the United States.[40]

Again, China's innovations in solar panel production are making renewable energy more and more competitive with conventional sources. And the country is busy developing modular construction techniques that allow green buildings to be put up in record time with reduced waste; China's Broad Group put up a thirty-story hotel in Changsha in fifteen days and is planning a 220-story skyscraper—the world's tallest—in the same city to be constructed in ninety days. The country's bullet train goes four and a half times faster than Amtrak's East Coast Acela train. The list goes on.

And it isn't just China and India that are innovating. Look at mobile banking. According to a recent global survey, there were twenty countries where more than one in ten adults used mobile money in 2012. Fifteen of those countries were in Africa. And the undoubted global leader was Kenya, where 68 percent of adults used mobile money in 2012.[41] That's just one more example of the global spread of innovation that is going to create new products and services from which everyone benefits—from Accra to Akron.

o o o

SO FAR WE HAVE FOCUSED on the links between brute economic factors in the global economy and the ways in which larger Chinese or Indian or Nigerian GDPs are likely to strengthen Western economies. There is considerably more to life than money, however. At least as exciting as the economic changes going on in the rest of the world are improvements in health and education and changing norms and values that suggest we're entering a healthier, more peaceful, and more cosmopolitan time for the planet. We're a long way from an end to history—a world free of war, plague, untimely death, discrimination, and bigotry—but we're a little closer to it, to the incredible benefit of us all.

Take the country at the tail end of the distribution in terms of developing-country success stories: the Democratic Republic of Congo (or DRC for short). After more than one hundred years of abuse, it is surely the most dysfunctional country on the planet. It started the twentieth century as the setting for Joseph Conrad's *Heart of Darkness,* under the brutal rule of King Leopold of Belgium, whose army was responsible for the deaths of hundreds of thousands through exploitation and disease. Independence in 1960 was accompanied by a vicious civil war and, soon thereafter, the rule of Mobutu Sese Seko—one of the most kleptocratic leaders in world history. His presidency ended in 1997 amid renewed civil conflict that continued into the new millennium and has now become the bloodiest war so far in the twenty-first century. Over the 1998 to 2007 period, that war killed somewhere between 1.8 million and 5.4 million people. The associated social disintegration has in places bordered on the medieval. In Kivu province in 2011, as many as forty women were raped every day—and one in ten contracted HIV as a result. Today the *average* income is around sixty-eight cents a day. That is, most Congolese are living for a week on the price of one McDonald's Happy Meal.[42]

But for all the immense suffering and regress on income in the DRC, in some ways even the "heart of darkness" isn't quite as nightmarish as it once was. Over the period 1990 to 2007, as war raged and poverty deepened, infant mortality rates dropped from 15 to 9 percent—still horribly high, but lower than rates in South Korea or Mexico in 1960. The proportion of underweight children declined. Maternal mortality also fell. Even HIV prevalence dropped, from 4.2 to 3.4 percent of the population.[43]

In no small part, these improvements are connected to the rollout of basic health services. Recent surveys suggest that nearly two-thirds of children are vaccinated against diphtheria, whooping cough, and tetanus, and more than half of all households have an insecticide-treated bed net. More than four out of ten kids who show symptoms of pneumonia receive antibiotics, and nearly the same proportion with symptoms of malaria are treated with antimalarial drugs. Those percentages forty years ago, when the country saw incomes three times as high as today's, were close to zero.[44]

And it isn't just health that has improved for the Congolese. Total school enrollment in the country reached 13 million students in 2007. The percentage of primary-age kids in school went from 64 to 84 percent from 2006 to 2008 alone, placing the enrollment rate in the DRC ahead of countries like Kuwait and Honduras as recently as 1980.

Given the state of the DRC economy, these achievements have been managed on a pittance. In 2009, according to the World Bank, health and education expenditure together accounted for around $9 per year per person in the DRC. That meager outlay, augmented by aid and the limited private resources available to individual citizens, has been enough to provide a level of health and schooling considerably better than would have been expected in far richer countries only a few years ago.

This progress even in the most desperate country on the planet is a sign of the absolute ubiquity of improvement in global quality of life worldwide over the past few decades. And that improvement has spillover effects. There were no cases of polio in the entire DRC in 2012, for example. That means the country is playing its part in the global battle to eradicate the disease. In 1952, more than 50,000 kids were paralyzed by a polio outbreak in the United States. If polio follows smallpox as the second human disease wiped off the face of the planet thanks to global collaboration, there will never again be the risk of a repeat of 1952.

Improved global vaccination performance in particular matters more and more to the old rich world because vaccination rates are going the *opposite* direction in the West. The vaccines are readily available and affordable in Europe and America, of course, but willfully ignorant parents aren't getting their kids protected. On a measure of global relative vaccination performance that looks at the sustained level of diphtheria, pertussis, and tetanus coverage over the period 1980 to 2010 developed by Amanda Glassman and her colleagues at the Center for Global Development, the United States ranked twenty-fourth, behind countries like Slovakia, Hungary, and Albania. France ranked thirty-first, and the United Kingdom ninety-first—behind Gambia and Eritrea.[45] In 2011, according to health economist Victoria Fan, France saw more than 14,000 cases of measles, the highest since 2000 and considerably above the total number of cases in the entirety of the Americas that year. And in the first nine months of 2012, the United States saw more cases of whooping cough than it had in decades, with 25,000 cases and thirteen deaths.[46] Particularly if we are going to allow Western parents to play roulette with their kids' lives, we've got to hope the rest of the world reduces the global risk of infectious disease by getting their kids vaccinated.

o   o   o

ONE OF THE MANY great things about a more educated planet is that higher education levels are a sign and symptom of a growing convergence in values against discrimination and in favor of cosmopolitanism. A global alignment toward greater tolerance will be a powerful force for both greater productivity and ever-closer integration—once more, to the benefit of us all.

Indeed, for all the talk of the global "clash of civilizations," the interesting thing about culture worldwide is how similar values already are across countries—and in many cases, the deepening convergence of those values. We're not about to see a world where everyone's a fan of Garth Brooks and understands the intricacies—or even just the point—of baseball. But cricket fans are less and less likely to get the pitchforks out if the new neighbors put up a Yankees banner.

India's caste system provides a powerful example of both how great the impact of culture on the quality of life can be and how rapid cultural change toward acceptance can occur, the caste traditionally known as "untouchables," make up a little under one-sixth of the country's population. Historically, they were limited to the performance of "unclean" tasks, like leatherwork and handling feces. Despite the fact that discrimination on the grounds of caste was banned by the country's independence constitution, and despite numerous government programs designed to ensure low-caste political representation and improve their social and economic status, discrimination has remained. Dalits and other "scheduled castes" remain less well-off across a range of measures of the quality of life.

Not least, people still overwhelmingly want to marry within their caste. Even low-caste teachers in India mark student tests lower when they know the students are low-caste, and Dalit students themselves perform worse on tests when reminded of their status before taking a test. After they leave school, low-caste graduates with the same qualifications earn less money. And Dalits are disproportionately poor and in bad health.[47]

But a paper by development economists Devesh Kapur, Chandra Bhan Prasad, Lant Pritchett, and Shyam Babu regarding Dalits suggests that for all that caste discrimination remains potent, it is considerably on the wane. A survey designed and led by members of the Dalit community in two areas of Uttar Pradesh found that attitudes and behaviors related to the low status of Dalits had been widely tempered or abandoned over the last twenty years. Dalit respondents reported that, since 1990, they have been far more likely to be seated next to high-caste guests at weddings rather than being seated separately, they are no longer expected to handle the dead animals of other castes, and non-Dalit midwives will attend births in Dalit households. They have moved in large numbers into nontraditional professions like tailoring and driving, and almost none participate in bonded labor for high-caste patrons anymore.[48]

Again, work by Tulane University's Myeong-Su Yun and his colleagues suggests that Dalits have seen dramatic shifts in their employment opportunities, so that, from 1983 to 2004, the proportion employed outside of agriculture climbed from 24 to 37 percent.[49]

The changes are huge. In Bulandshahr district, fewer than 4 percent of Dalits said that non-Dalits would accept food in their household in 1990, but nearly half said that they would today. In 1990, nearly three-quarters of respondents suggested that only Dalits handled dead animals—that fraction in 2007 was one in twenty. The proportion who suggested that most or all girls in a household went to school in 1990 was 7 percent—at the time of the survey that had climbed to 57 percent.

Dalits are considerably wealthier now than they were in 1990. Kapur and his colleagues suggest, however, that the social transformation is far too dramatic to be accounted for by income changes alone. "This is not to suggest," they caution, "that caste has disappeared as a social construct. It is very much alive." Nonetheless, Dalits have seen both far greater prosperity, "*and* the social and cultural fabric of the village has changed, much for the better," they conclude.[50]

And it isn't just caste in India, of course. The World Values Survey is a global poll that reports attitudes toward topics from religion to democracy, gender roles, and politics. Across countries that took part in the 1993 to 1998 wave and the 2004 to 2006 wave of the World Values Survey, only 13 percent of respondents in the average country suggested that they did not want to live next to a person of a different race in the 2004 to 2006 wave. This was down from 17 percent in the 1993 to 1998 wave. Three-quarters of the countries surveyed in both waves saw this measure of racism decline. The average proportion of respondents across countries saying that they didn't want to live next to someone of a different religion fell from 44 to 33 percent—with declining rates of religious intolerance on this measure in 91 percent of surveyed countries. And between the 1993 to 1998 wave and the 2004 to 2006 wave, the average proportion saying that homosexuality is never justifiable fell from 59 to 34 percent, with declines in 93 percent of surveyed countries. That still adds up to a world with potentially billions of bigots (especially as some large countries remain less tolerant), but almost everywhere bigotry is both on the wane and already the minority view.[51]

Again, a recent Council on Foreign Relations report has gathered data on global opinions related to human rights that suggest widespread tolerance and fellow-feeling. An average of 86 percent of respondents across twenty-one developed and developing countries said that it's important for women to have full equality of rights with men, and the same poll suggested that equality of treatment for different races and ethnicities was important to an average of 91 percent of respondents across countries. A 2007 survey of twenty-four countries, including Kenya, Nigeria, China, India, Germany, and the United States, found that, in every country, the great majority of respondents thought it is important to treat people of different religions equally. Even in the lowest-scoring country (Egypt), 74 percent agreed that this is very or somewhat important.[52]

Or take views on democracy, as reflected in the World Values Survey of countries across the globe. The percentage of national populations who thought that having a democratic political system is a good thing was 98 percent in Egypt, 94 percent in China, 93 percent in Vietnam, 92 percent in Iran, and 88 percent in Iraq. Some countries were less sold on the idea of democratic systems—in the United States, only 86 percent of the population voiced support for such a system. But in every country where the question was asked, considerable majorities backed democracy. Across the countries surveyed from 2004 to 2006, the average was 87 percent support for democracy as the best form of government.[53]

There is more to democracy than the vote, and more to the reality of democracy than theoretical support voiced in surveys. In 1997, Fareed Zakaria coined the term "illiberal democracies" to describe the phenomenon of democratic governments running amok over civil rights.[54] And recent events in the Middle East suggest the considerable potential for such regimes to emerge there. While Islamic and Western countries score almost exactly the same in popular opinion polls when it comes to attitudes toward democracy and democratic ideals, note Pippa Norris of Harvard and Ronald Inglehart of the University of Michigan, support for gender equality, divorce, and abortion is notably lower, and support for homosexuality hardly registers.[55] Again, recent violence against Coptic Christians in Egypt and proposed legislation further limiting women's rights suggest that Egypt—along with many other countries—has a long way to go in converting theoretical opinions into practical protections. Nonetheless, support for—and implementation of—universal suffrage suggest at least some movement toward the idea of the equal value of persons.[56]

And behavior change suggests that there is more to the poll evidence than parroting fashionable opinion. Preferences across a range of issues really are converging across the planet. Think about changing attitudes toward kids. There's no evidence at all that people are having less sex, but a lot fewer babies are being produced as a result of it. The total fertility rate in Spain was cut in half between 1970 and 1990, for example, but it wasn't just Spain: women the world over, whether rich or poor, educated or not, or religious or doubting, appear to have decided that life would be better with fewer kids, and more women have the power within the household to enact that decision. The average number of kids a woman has in the developing world fell from 5.4 to 2.7 between 1970 and today. Countries from Iran to Vietnam already have fertility rates low enough to suggest that local populations are likely to shrink over time, and global fertility rates are converging in that direction.[57]

Again, and doubtless related, is the fact that the "new normal" the world over is parents sending their girls to school. In Ethiopia in 1996, there were only around six girls in school for every ten boys, according to World Bank data. By 2010, that had climbed to nearly a nine-to-ten ratio. The progress in Ethiopia was particularly fast, but it was part of a strong worldwide trend.[58] You can't explain the increase in female secondary enrollment in low- and middle-income countries from 42 to 50 percent over the past decade without a story that involves rapidly, dramatically shifting values when it comes to the importance of educating girls.

And once again, democratic attitudes are more and more reflected in democratic realities. The Polity IV Project database, maintained by George Mason University, rates the world's countries on their status on a spectrum between absolute autocracy and perfect democracy. The average global Polity score across countries has never been as high as it is today, nor has the percentage of countries getting a perfect score. The number of countries that are broadly democratic has doubled since the start of the 1980s. In terms of gender and racial equality, in 1970 thirty countries—including Switzerland—did not extend voting rights to all adult citizens. By 2010, only four countries still limited full suffrage. Democracy is now the default for political systems worldwide.[59]

What accounts for this global convergence in values? Doubtless growing urbanization and increasing educational levels play a role—more liberal attitudes have long been associated with higher enrollment rates and city living. Technologies have also played a part in spurring cultural convergence. One of the more amusing

WikiLeaks revelations involved a cable from the US embassy in Riyadh, reporting on a conversation between diplomats and TV directors in Saudi Arabia about the comparative impact of the US government–funded channel in the country (al-Hurrah) compared to the local Rupert Murdoch–owned channel. No one really cared for the long interviews with George Bush broadcast on al-Hurrah (at a cost to the US taxpayer of $500 million—considerably more than the budget of *Sesame Street*). But, reported the diplomats, the Saudi director suggested that the broadcasts by Murdoch's MBC 4 channel of *Friends* and *David Letterman,* among other US cultural icons, were popular even in remote, conservative areas of the country.[60] This echoes findings from research in Brazil and India: as television signals rolled out across those countries, women's decision-making power increased and girls' school enrollment rates climbed, among other impacts.[61]

And technology-enabled cross-cultural conversation is becoming increasingly straightforward, suggesting that the attitude and behavioral changes are likely to continue. The proportion of the world with Internet access climbed from 6.4 percent in 2000 to 29.7 percent in 2010. About 42 percent of those users in 2010 were in Asia, and there were more Internet users in China than in the United States. With close to universal mobile phone access likely by 2030, and with the increasing power of mobile devices, the Internet will become the most widespread idea dissemination tool of all, overtaking broadcast television and radio. It's a tool for disseminating bigoted rants, to be sure, but to date, communication has been more closely associated with converging global values.

We're hardly at the point of global comity and the end of national differences. Pippa Norris and Ronald Inglehart point out that the World Values Survey shows no consistent decline in nationalism across countries, for example.[62] And the convergence of values doesn't necessarily translate into a convergence on American values. In part that's because American values themselves have undergone considerable change over time, especially on issues like the environment and homosexuality. Perhaps we're really all converging on the Norse norms of Scandinavia. But with growing cosmopolitanism in the United States and around the world, trade, investment, travel, and migration across borders are all made easier, and the risk of global misunderstanding—and resulting violence—may be reduced as well. The potential for clashing civilizations is distinctly on the decline.

o o o

INDEED, RELATED TO A GROWING global acceptance of people with different creeds, colors, or nationalities has been a widespread reduction in violence. In 2001, homicide was responsible for more than twice as many deaths worldwide as deaths in wars (an estimated 557,000 people, compared to total war deaths of around 208,000), but violent crime rates have been falling across not only the West but a large part of the rest of the planet. The data are patchy, but in 2002 about 332,000 homicides in ninety-four countries were reported to the UN. By 2008 that number had dropped to 289,000. And from 2002 to 2008, the homicide rate fell in sixty-eight reporting countries and increased in only twenty-six.[63]

Meanwhile, the number of wars of all kinds ongoing worldwide, which increased from five in 1961 to twenty-four in 1984, had dropped back to five again by 2008. Battle deaths in war have also fallen considerably, according to Bethany Lacina and Nils Gleditsch, researchers from the Center for the Study of Civil

War.[64] The average annual number of battle deaths per international conflict dropped from 21,000 in the 1950s to fewer than 3,000 in the new millennium, according to the Human Security Report. "Today's armed conflicts rarely generate enough fatalities to reverse the long-term downward trend in peacetime mortality," suggests the report.[65]

There is still far too much death and destruction around—including in the Democratic Republic of Congo. But the trend is strongly in the right direction. And there are a number of reasons to believe that it will continue that way. Continued convergence in values and the growth in democracy will be two factors. Democracies only infrequently war with other democracies—and haven't done so at all since World War I. They have also been less likely to engage in mass killings in the last one hundred years.[66]

Another factor, as we have seen, is that war just makes less and less economic sense for superpowers—and that's a finding that holds more generally. In 1999, Thomas Friedman noted in *The Lexus and the Olive Tree* that no two countries that both have a McDonald's have gone to war. When Russia opened its first McDonald's in 1990, the number of countries worldwide serving Big Macs was only around forty. Since then, sixty-five countries have joined the Coalition of the McWilling. Although naysayers might note that Russia and Georgia both had an outlet before the South Ossetia conflict, and that a McDonald's-rich NATO alliance was willing to bomb Serbia—which had a McDonald's of its own—these are minor exceptions that prove the rule. Friedman's broader point that the increasing strength of global economic ties makes war less attractive seems borne out by considerable research.[67] For example, Carlos Seiglie and his colleagues argue that trade and foreign direct investment between countries is associated with a decreased chance of a war breaking out—and there has been a lot more foreign investment of late.[68]

A reduced chance of unrest or war is one more reason why the West should be happy about the rise of the Rest. "Fragile states"—those that are in conflict, or are at risk of conflict—are a major security concern to Western nations, not least because they may harbor international terrorists or pose risks, from the diseases they may be harboring to the crops they may be raising for the drug trade. If the rise of the Rest reduces the number of such countries, converting them into stable trade and investment partners, risks to continued progress in the West will be that much lower.

○ ○ ○

ALL OF THIS GREATER global peace and togetherness will be one reason the world is increasingly merry. The proportion of the planet reporting that they were somewhat or very happy climbed from under three-quarters to over four-fifths between the 1993 to 1998 and 2004 to 2006 World Values Survey waves.[69] It may be that contentment has declined since 2005 as a result of the financial crisis. But Princeton economist Angus Deaton suggests that happiness polls have pretty much recovered their pre-crisis levels in the United States. And countries like China and India, which make up much of the global population, didn't see recession over the past few years. So it seems very likely that cheer remains the default state for an ever-greater majority of humanity.[70]

That's as it should be. Everyone should be happy about the immense opportunities presented by the new wealth of emerging economies, especially the considerable preponderance of the world's population who live in those economies. And the West ought to be encouraging that growth: it is in the self-interest of North America and Europe that Asia and Africa and Latin America continue getting richer, healthier, more educated, and more cosmopolitan.

And it is particularly in the West's interest if the Rest continues to outpace Western history when it comes to concern over the environment. Because if there is one way in which the rise of the Rest really does pose a challenge to the West, it is through its growing share of demands on the global commons — notably the atmosphere. That is the subject of the next chapter.

CHAPTER FIVE

Will Greater Wealth Destroy the Planet?

W E HAVE SEEN THAT A RANGE of values appear to be converging worldwide, and one of them is concern for the environment. Even in the United States, popular opinion is now behind doing something about climate change. Americans are far from being completely sold on the issue: more than 60 percent also support more offshore drilling and (among those who have heard of it) two-thirds want to build the Keystone XL pipeline to transport tar sands bitumen from Canada to oil refineries on the US Gulf coast. Nonetheless, three-quarters of the public support tax rebates for people who buy fuel-efficient vehicles or solar panels and the regulation of carbon dioxide as a pollutant, and according to George Mason University polling, nearly two-thirds of Americans even support an international treaty requiring the United States to cut carbon dioxide emissions by 90 percent by 2050. Ask people the world over if they are willing to give up part of their income for the environment, and according to the World Values Survey, two-thirds say yes—including 82 percent of people in China, 68 percent of people in India, and (even) 52 percent of Americans.[1]

This is good news, because there really are serious threats to planetary prosperity posed by our overuse of natural resources and exacerbated by the rise of the Rest. There are two concerns here. First, if it's a resource that comes out of the ground, somebody, somewhere, has probably suggested that it has peaked—or is about to do so. Extraction will become too costly to continue at current rates, with awesome economic consequences. But as worldwide reserves of mineral resources continue to climb and new technologies suggest the potential for North America to become an energy-exporting region, a second concern looms large: not running out of resources but having too many for the planet's own good. And that highlights a big potential stumbling block to rapid progress toward an ever-wealthier world: the global climate.

That second threat is almost certainly the more immediate one to continued growth in global prosperity. But the good news is that it is not too late to act—climate change that is effectively locked in by our past decisions will not be so disruptive as to significantly slow planetary progress. So if we accelerate toward a low-carbon global economy, the future looks bright. And the better news is that countries from both the West and the Rest are at last starting to do something serious about the issue.

o   o   o

DURING THE TWENTIETH CENTURY, global economic output went up about twentyfold, but demand for some resources climbed considerably faster than that. And yet commodity prices fell, owing to new technologies, new finds, and the changing pattern of demand for resources. Over the last century of historically unprecedented global mineral extraction, industrial commodity prices declined by an average of around 70 percent. There were spikes, of course—especially around World War I and the 1970s oil shock. And we are in a price spike now.[2] *The Economist*'s index of non-oil commodity prices has trebled in the past decade. But prices are still only at about half the level they were between 1845 and 1920—when we were extracting perhaps one-twentieth as much planetwide per year as we are today.[3]

What has driven price changes over the long term is that downward pressure on prices from advances in production technologies has outweighed upward pressure due to both extraction of the most easily accessible deposits and increased demand. Over the past twenty years, a sudden expansion in demand, fostered by the most rapid global exit out of mass poverty ever, has pushed prices up. Indeed, China alone experienced growth that had it accounting for nearly half of global consumption of iron ore and around 40 percent of lead, zinc, aluminum, copper, and nickel by 2010, up from a small fraction of that twenty years earlier.[4] But supply is responding—and there are plenty of supplies out there.

Take petroleum. In 1978 President Jimmy Carter warned in his televised address on the energy crisis that "we could use up all the proven reserves of oil in the entire world by the end of the next decade"—in other words, by 1990.[5] But more than two decades after 1990, *oil reserves worldwide keep on growing.* In the years 2007 to 2009, for every barrel of oil produced in the world, 1.6 barrels of new reserves were added. So considerable are recent discoveries in Canada and the United States that, between them, the two countries might actually come close to that

Washingtonian holy grail of "energy independence" by 2035, with no need for the United States to import a single barrel from the Middle East. The World Energy Council reports that global proven recoverable reserves of natural gas liquids and crude oil amounted to 1.2 trillion barrels in 2010—or thirty-eight years' worth at current usage. Add in shale oil resources and that's another 4.8 trillion barrels, or a century and a half at present usage rates—if we can figure out economical ways to extract it. Tar sands, including some huge Canadian deposits, add an immense amount more—perhaps 6 trillion barrels.[6]

And it isn't just oil. From aluminum to zirconium, global mineral resources are proving more than adequate to meet demand for a long time to come. Look at copper. A British study from as long ago as the 1930s predicted an acute global shortage of the metal "within a generation." Not so much.[7] According to data from the US Geological Survey, in 1970 world copper reserves were estimated to be 280 million tons. In 2010, thanks to new finds and technological advances, copper reserves were more than double the 1970 estimates—despite the fact that we'd mined 400 million tons of the stuff in the meantime.[8]

Today's copper reserves would last for only thirty-nine years at current production levels. But there's still no need to panic: reserves are only a partial measure of what's sitting in the ground to be extracted in that they quantify known deposits of a mineral that could be economically produced today. Global *resource* statistics estimate how much of a mineral is *potentially* feasible to extract worldwide. If you are worried about "running out" of copper, then, it is the resource number that's of most interest. And land-based resources are estimated at 3 billion tons or more—or 185,000 years at current production levels. Even better news, that's almost double the estimate of resources from eleven years ago—so perhaps the number has further to climb. And when we do finally run out of land-based supplies, there are still the undersea sources to use up.

Concerns over phosphate, vital to fertilizer production, came to the fore as prices for the rock rose sixfold in early 2008. Prices declined rapidly thereafter, but remained at about double their level in the early part of the decade. Nonetheless, the long-term picture is reassuring: estimated global phosphate reserves climbed from 11 million tons in 1995 to 65 million tons in 2010—and that's equal to 369 years of current production.

Meanwhile, Japan has recently discovered 6.8 million tons of the rare earth minerals vital to the electronics industry—200 years' worth of the country's current consumption—in its Pacific seabed. A range of other countries are also bringing production online. While China currently supplies 90 percent of the world's output of rare earths, that situation will soon change. The list goes on: resource estimates by the US Geological Survey suggest global beryllium reserves equal to about 890 years of current annual production levels, 347 years for helium, centuries for chromium, and more than a millennium for lithium and strontium. And for those worried about peak cosmetics or the ugly effect of makeup embargoes against the United States, talc resources in the United States alone could provide over a thousand years of supplies at current rates of domestic production.[9]

Added to the good news, expanding global reserve estimates reflect rising stocks in a lot of poor countries, thanks to recent discoveries of significant oil fields and mineral concentrations. A growing number of developing countries are likely to earn money from drilling and mining, following in the footsteps of countries like Ghana (on the cusp of an oil boom) and Mongolia (ramping up its copper exports). And for those worried by the "resource curse"—the idea that development of oil and mining industries predestines a country to dictatorship and poverty—recent analysis by the World Bank and other researchers suggests that the fear of the curse is overblown; "as one might intuitively expect, greater natural resource wealth is associated with higher GDP per capita," concludes the World Bank report dryly.[10]

Meanwhile, the US Geological Survey points us to another reason to downplay fears of global economic collapse brought on by wells running dry or mines hitting the end of the seam: substitutes for minerals. Take copper, for example: you can substitute aluminum for copper in power cables and electrical equipment. In fact, technological change has already dampened growing demand for copper because no self-respecting telecom company uses the metal in new wires anymore—fiber optics carry so much more traffic in the same-size cable.

Such changes happen a lot over time. In 1865 war erupted among Spain, Peru, and Chile over the control of islands strategically important because of their considerable stocks of guano. The substance—dried bird poop—was a source of fertilizer as well as nitrates for gunpowder at the time. But guano is rarely used on fields today, nor does the Department of Defense stockpile it for production of cruise missiles or depleted uranium shells.

If we keep on using more minerals and don't do a better job of recycling them, and if plans to mine the moon don't work out, we'll run out of supplies one day. There is only so much rock in the planet, after all. But for pretty much every vital mineral resource, that day looks to be some way off, however fast the developing world grows. That's good news for the world economy, of course—and good news for the West.

o   o   o

BUT WHAT ABOUT SUFFICIENT LAND and fresh water to feed a growing—and more affluent—world population? Over the next fifty years, food output will have to rise 50 percent to feed two billion extra people and their growing appetite for meat. And this while one-third of the world's population already faces water shortages and, by 2030, one-third of the world could live in areas where the gap between water needs and an accessible, reliable supply is greater than 50 percent.[11]

But before predicting famines of proportions that would make an Old Testament scribe salivate, it is worth noting that between 1967 and 2007, global crop yields grew by an estimated 115 percent. The "green revolution" in India doubled wheat production between 1964 and 1970 alone. And in the developing world as a whole over the first eight years of the new century, cereal yields increased at about twice the rate of population growth. That's why the price of rice, even at the height of the food price spike of 2008, remained one-half to one-third its level forty years earlier.[12]

Looking forward, while the rate of progress needed to increase output to meet global demand must be slightly higher than long-term trends, it need not be considerably higher. A team led by Jonathan Foley of the University of Minnesota wrote in the journal *Nature* that global food production could be doubled by intensifying production in regions where yields are low through fertilizer, irrigation, and other productivity gains.[13] In Africa, for example, yields per hectare for cereals are perhaps one-eighth or less of technological potential and around one-quarter of average yields in China. That could change rapidly. Take Malawi, where a program of subsidies for improved maize seed and fertilizers over the last few years increased national maize production by 50 percent. Farmers in the country supplied with adequate fertilizer and hybrid seed can produce five tons on a hectare plot, compared to one ton using traditional methods.[14]

The *Nature* team also notes that further efficiency gains could be accomplished in high-yield regions by *lower* resource use.[15] Already, in the club of OECD rich countries between 1990 and 2004, food production increased 5 percent and agricultural biodiversity improved while agricultural land shrank by 4 percent and soil erosion, greenhouse gas emissions, and excessive fertilizer use all declined. And seed industry projections—for all of their potential biases—suggest that improved breeding and biotechnology could double US maize yields between 2005 and 2030.[16]

And with regard to water, there are a number of methods to dramatically, and very cheaply, increase water efficiency at a considerably more aggressive rate than the 1 percent a year we've managed for the past couple of decades. Both no-till farming (avoiding the plow) and better management of irrigation can have a dramatic impact on water use. A recent McKinsey study estimates the total global cost to ensure sufficient water for agriculture worldwide in 2030 to be $50 billion to $60 billion a year—only around 0.06 percent of GDP at that point.[17]

And expanding agricultural trade amounts to trade in water (as does trade in other goods that take a lot of water to produce). Already, "embedded water" in traded products accounts for about one-fifth of the global annual water footprint of humanity. The 40 million tons of grain exported to the Middle East from the European Union and the United States in 1998 took about 40 billion tons of water to produce—equal to the annual flow of the Nile. More agricultural and industrial imports will allow water-scarce areas to prosper and sustain their populations by trading with rain-drenched partners.[18]

Greater wealth, stronger global yields, and a global food trade and aid system are why famines have become increasingly rare of late. Famines are "so easy to prevent that it is amazing that they are allowed to occur at all," in the words of Nobel Prize–winning economist Amartya Sen.[19] In fact, famines don't occur anymore in any place where leaders show the slightest concern for the well-being of their citizenry. And in turn, that might help explain why the link between weather and civil unrest is weak. For example, a 2008 review of the evidence linking climate to conflict in the *Journal of Peace Research* suggested that "claims of environmental determinism leading seamlessly from climate change to open warfare are suspect."[20]

Related good news is that recent reestimates of global hunger suggest that poor people were less susceptible to past price spikes than we had previously thought. The old numbers from the Food and Agricultural Organization reported undernourishment climbing from 790 million to a little over one billion from 1995 to 2009 as food prices rose. The new numbers—themselves still far from a perfect measure—suggest that there were in fact closer to one billion malnourished people in 1995, but that the number *dropped* to 870 million during the food price hikes, thanks to growing wealth and better safety nets.

Finally, there is still a lot of slack in the system. One-third of food production is simply wasted worldwide—spoiled before it reaches consumers or thrown away after it does. Again, a growing proportion of crops are used to feed the animals that end up as special-sauced patties between sesame seed buns. All of that meat-eating is an incredibly inefficient way to provide nutrition as well as one factor behind the global obesity epidemic. If people in rich and middle-income countries did the healthy thing and ate less meat, that would not only help tackle an overweight problem for one billion people worldwide but also reduce the price of basic foodstuffs for the world's poorest consumers.

In all likelihood, undernutrition will continue to decline as a concern even while the obesity epidemic worsens. The big public health challenge around food over the next fifty years will be discovering not how the planet can grow enough to prevent mass starvation, but how to avoid letting fat become the number-one killer. As with resources from out of the ground, so with resources grown on the ground—overconsumption is likely to be the greater threat in the medium term than lack of resources.

o   o   o

IN FACT, FOR ALL THE GOOD NEWS about global mineral reserves and the hope for expanding agricultural output, this planetary cornucopia does present a significant challenge. Were we to continue expanding our resource use at current rates, we would pollute our way to a denuded planet. Mining, drilling, and moving industrial commodities is a messy business. Remember the *Exxon Valdez* and the Gulf of Mexico oil spills? Or look at the mountaintops removed in the Appalachians to feed our hunger for coal. That's to say nothing of the impact on the global climate. The tar sand fields in Alberta, Canada, alone contain 1.73 trillion barrels, give or take a half-century of current global oil use, but it is an environmentalist's nightmare to produce it. Two tons of tar sands are needed to produce every barrel of oil. Getting the sludgelike stuff to the surface takes pumping steam into the tar beds, which in turn takes burning gas. So it takes greenhouse gases to produce and emits more when it is burned.

Intensive farming also uses a lot of energy and resources, so the demands of a richer planet to produce more food (let alone more cars, iPads, and McMansions) add considerably to the stresses on the global commons—and in particular the atmosphere. Were nine billion people to consume resources in anything like the way the one billion do in the West today, the environmental costs would be catastrophic.

All of which makes it disappointing that international agreements to protect the environment appear to have had such limited impact. Take the Kyoto Protocol, the only global agreement that actually binds some countries to reductions in their greenhouse gas emissions. It binds none of the world's three largest polluters, which among them are responsible for nearly half of all emissions. That's because the United States never signed the Protocol, while India and China, as developing countries, were exempted from emissions caps on the grounds that the rich countries have done the majority of the combusting, excreting, or otherwise expelling of the gases that has caused the atmosphere such heartburn to date.

Worse, while the Kyoto agreement has been limpidly extended, a replacement won't be in place until after 2015. And bargaining positions are hardening: experts reporting to a group of developing countries that includes China and India have suggested that developed countries like the United States and those in Europe should be absorbing more carbon dioxide than they emit over the next few years—which would be quite the technical challenge. We could call our progress toward a global binding agreement glacial, except that in fact we're going backward (and glaciers are actually falling into the sea quite fast nowadays).[21] Overall, disheartening progress typifies the results of global environmental treaty-making, from biodiversity through forests to fish stocks.

There is plenty to be gloomy about—particularly if you are a polar bear or a farmer in the Sahel. But it's important to put climate change and other global environmental challenges in a broader context. They are vital global issues — ones that threaten to slow the worldwide march toward improved quality of life. Climate change alone is already responsible for more extreme weather and an accelerating rate of species extinction, and it may ultimately kill off as many as 40 percent of all living species. Unchecked, climate change will add to our agricultural challenges over the course of the century. A 2001 Intergovernmental Panel on Climate Change (IPCC) report estimated that climate change over the very long term could reduce agricultural yields by as much as 30 percent.[22]

But these are also problems that we know how to tackle and that are not so bad (yet) that they are likely to completely derail progress at the global or national level. Which is good news: that these issues are manageable is the best reason to try to tackle them rather than abandon all hope.

Start with the economic impact of climate change that is effectively inevitable because of our slow response to date. The *Stern Review*, commissioned by the British Treasury from Nicholas Stern (at that point head of the UK Government Economic Service), is the most comprehensive look to date at the economics of climate change. It suggests that, in terms of income, greenhouse gases are a threat to global growth, but not an immediately catastrophic one. Take the impact of climate change on the developing world. The most depressing forecast in terms of developing-country growth in Stern's paper is the "A2 scenario," a model that predicts slow global growth and income convergence. But even under this model, Afghanistan's GDP per capita will climb sixfold over the next ninety years, India's and China's ninefold, and Ethiopia's income will increase by a factor of ten. Knock off one-third for the most pessimistic simulation of the economic impact of climate change suggested by the *Stern Review* and people in those countries are still markedly better off—four times as rich for Afghanistan, a little more than six times as rich for Ethiopia—than they are today.[23]

And poor people become more resilient to the effects of climate change as they become wealthier. For example, as the continent's economy grew, agriculture's share of Africa's GDP fell from 22 to 13 percent between 1967 and 2009.[24] The less the economy relies on agriculture—and in particular non-irrigated agriculture—the less it depends on rainfall or cool weather.

The comparatively limited impact of climate change on global economic growth over the next few decades is why a recent World Bank analysis of the likely impact of global warming on poverty between now and midcentury concluded that "the expected poverty impact will be relatively modest and far from reversing the major decline in poverty that is expected to occur over the next 40 years as a result of continued economic growth." The report suggested that the proportion of the world living on less than $2 a day would fall from 32.3 percent in 2005 to 14.1 percent in 2055 absent climate change, and to 14.2 percent factoring in the effects of global warming.[25]

What about the impact of climate change on global health? The World Health Organization's analysis suggests that the limited warming that has already occurred is responsible for 140,000 deaths annually owing to the spread of diseases, including malaria and dengue fever, among other impacts. Most of the vectors for such diseases—mosquitoes, biting flies, and so on—do poorly in frost. So if the weather stays warmer, one could conclude, these diseases are likely to spread. But worldwide we have seen declining deaths and reduced malarial spread over the last century, particularly in Africa over the last ten years.[26]

The authors of a recent study published in the journal *Nature* conclude that the forecasted future effects of rising temperatures on malaria "are at least one order of magnitude smaller than the changes observed since about 1900 and about two orders of magnitude smaller than those that can be achieved by the effective scale-up of key control measures."[27] Douglas Gollin at Williams College and Christian Zimmermann at the University of Connecticut have evaluated the likely impact of a three-degree rise in temperatures on tropical diseases like dengue fever, which causes 22,000 deaths each year. They suggest that the rollout of existing public health tools would more than compensate for the effects of a warmer, wetter climate.[28]

And while climate change will make extreme weather events and natural disasters like flooding and hurricanes more common, the negative effect on global quality of life will be reduced if economies continue to grow. That's because the vast majority of deaths by natural disaster occur in poor countries. The more money people and governments have, the more they can both afford and enforce building codes, land use regulations, and public infrastructure like flood defenses, all of which can lower death tolls.[29]

So the impacts of a level of climate change already effectively locked in by past carbon dioxide emissions and unavoidable future emissions are pretty grim: perhaps ten million more worldwide will live in poverty over the next few decades, and hundreds of thousands more may die, than would have been the case without climate change. And the longer-term consequences of inaction—a four-degree warmer world, as it might be—may be orders of magnitude larger. The economic case for responding to climate change by taxing carbon emissions and investing in nonpolluting energy sources *today* is clear. But for all the world will be a considerably poorer, denuded place in the long term if we do not respond rapidly to reduce greenhouse gases, the global economy is likely to continue to expand over the next few decades, and global health is likely to continue to improve, even allowing for the impact of locked-in climate change.[30]

A second reason for hope about the future is that a big, complex global treaty like a follow-up to Kyoto isn't the only way to deal with big, complex global problems. Myriad individual countries are already responding to the threat. In fact, action by a small number of countries acting in the planetary interest may baffle economists and international relations experts alike, but it has actually driven most of the progress in tackling global issues to date. To paraphrase Margaret Mead, never doubt that a small group of committed states can change the world; indeed, it's the only thing that usually does. Think of the great acts of discovery bankrolled by the Spanish crown to cross the Atlantic, the Soviet Union putting a man in space, the US Defense Department creating the Internet, and the European states financing particle physics at CERN (European Organization for Nuclear Research). Or what about the British campaign in the nineteenth century to wipe out the Atlantic slave trade, a vital step in the global abolition of a most peculiar, evil institution? US funding of the global smallpox eradication drive saved hundreds of millions of lives worldwide. And more recently, think about the informal alliance of countries that has come together to protect global sea-lanes from the threat of piracy.

The good news is that a similar global response to climate change has already started. In fact, greenhouse gas emissions caps have been behind a notable slowing of carbon dioxide output across Europe. EU carbon dioxide emissions fell by 6 percent between 1991 and 2007, for example. Even the United States—a pariah in the Kyoto discussions, blamed for stymieing progress toward a global agreement—has taken some stumbling steps in the right direction. In 2011, US carbon dioxide emissions had fallen back to their 1996 level despite output that was 40 percent higher, thanks in large part to the fact that coal's share of electricity production fell from 50 percent to 40 percent from 2008 to 2012. That share is predicted to fall further, to 30 percent, by 2020.[31]

One big factor behind this change is increased energy production from domestic gas supplies produced by hydraulic fracturing, or "fracking." The approach raises its own environmental concerns: lubricants, along with the natural gas and other compounds from methane, benzene, xylene, carbon disulfide, naphthalene, and pyridines, sometimes escape into local water supplies or the atmosphere. But domestic gas's rapidly growing share of electricity production shows that the energy mix in the United States can change pretty rapidly under the right circumstances—which is good news for those worried about the legacy impact of current power plant construction on future efforts to reduce emissions. And coal's decline is also linked to tighter clean air regulations, activism against coal plant construction, and the rise of clean energy, supported by twenty-nine state-level mandatory renewable energy standards.

Meanwhile, the federal government has set new fuel economy standards that will increase the average energy efficiency of America's automobiles by about one-half by 2025. And California is under an executive order to cut greenhouse gas emissions to 80 percent below their 1990 level by 2050. That really matters because California's economy is still larger than Russia's or India's (at market exchange rates). The state is also home to considerable research capacity. So if California creates demand for low-carbon technologies, that's going to foster a lot of clean-tech development.[32]

More good news is that developing countries are also taking considerable action to curb carbon emissions. At the UN global warming confab at Cancun, Mexico, in 2010, developing countries pledged to restrict their carbon emissions more than did rich-country delegations. In particular, China's promised reductions from what would happen under "business as usual" were a lot larger than promises made by the United States. And that's very important considering that while the United States accounts for three times as much carbon dioxide already pumped into the atmosphere as China, today China is the largest carbon emitter in the world. India and the rest of the developing world are fast climbing the ranks as well. Without developing-country leadership, we'd all be sunk (literally, in the case of Vanuatu).

China's fuel economy standards for vehicles were around 25 percent tougher than US rules until recent Obama administration reforms. China generated 667 terawatt-hours of electricity from hydro, wind, and nuclear sources in 2009, a 50 percent increase from four years earlier (and more than one hundred times the state of Vermont's annual electricity consumption). China already accounts for one-quarter of the world's installed capacity in wind, small-hydro, biomass, solar, geothermal, and marine power facilities. And the overall amount of energy used to produce a dollar of GDP in China has dropped 5 percent every year since 1980, according to Qi Ye at the Climate Policy Initiative in Beijing.[33] The country has already launched a pilot carbon-trading scheme (firms buying permits that allow them to emit carbon dioxide into the atmosphere) and may roll it out countrywide by 2020.

It isn't just China. India has plans to generate 15 percent of its energy from renewable energy sources that don't emit carbon as early as 2020, primarily from solar power plants. And developing countries as a whole accounted for two-thirds of the growth in renewable and nuclear power–generating capacity worldwide from 2002 to 2008, according to David Wheeler at the Center for Global Development. The developing world is now home to more than half of the world's renewable energy–generating capacity, and it is likely to extend that lead.[34]

And there are lots of reasons to believe that we can speed progress to a low-carbon economy without considerable costs to growth. Not least, the amount of oil needed to produce a dollar of output is already declining. Each four dollars of global output worldwide took energy supplies equivalent to a kilogram of oil to produce in 1980. By 2009, we produced more than five dollars of output for the same amount of energy input.

Meanwhile, technology advance continues to make clean energy ever more competitive. A recent report from the United Nations Industrial Development Organization notes that the prices of photovoltaic modules, used to produce solar power, have been falling at a rate of 15 to 24 percent a year for some time. Prices charged by developers for solar projects have dropped even lower: recent contracts for solar power provision in the United States have seen an upper-end price of just nine cents per kilowatt-hour—not much different from coal-fired plants. As early as 2009, the California Energy Commission rejected a contract for a new gas-fired power plant in San Diego on the basis that a PV solar system would lower the cost of electricity for rate-payers.[35]

At the household level in the developed world, countries with higher electricity prices, like Germany, Italy, and Spain, have already reached "socket parity"—investing in a home solar system will provide a 5 percent or greater return in savings from the utility bill. As solar prices drop, more and more countries will reach socket parity. In many countries where the weather is slightly brighter than the gloom of a German winter and where the grid connecting customers to coal power plants hasn't been built, the cost-competiveness of home solar will be even greater.

These declining costs are a major factor behind an explosion in use. A report by the Natural Resources Defense Council calculates that in just the five years from 2006 to 2011, wind, solar, geothermal, tidal, and wave electricity production increased from 1 percent to 2.7 percent of total US production, from 0.1 percent to 1.5 percent in China, and from 5.3 percent to 10.7 percent in Germany. One sunny Saturday in May 2012 saw Germany produce nearly half of its electricity from solar. Given the long life of power plants—often measured in decades—this rate of change is phenomenal. Again, five years ago, total global photovoltaic capacity was just 16 gigawatts. In 2011 alone, the world added nearly twice that—29 gigawatts of new capacity. The United States, China, and the European Union between them invested $133 billion in clean energy in 2011, with China alone accounting for $50 billion of that. While investment slowed in 2012, the outlook for renewables remains very bright.[36]

o o o

IT IS TRUE THAT THE INITIATIVES to date in the battle against climate change are not yet nearly enough to stop global warming at below two degrees Centigrade, the internationally agreed target. All of the pledges made by various countries to cut greenhouse gas emissions so far (even were they met) amount to less than half of what scientists suggest is needed. And local initiatives backed by (hopefully rapid) technology change still remain a second-best to leaders from rich and poor countries alike, showing actual leadership by agreeing to a binding global treaty with greenhouse gas emissions caps for all countries.

But, again, the good news for the planet is that the rest of the world—including developing countries and the US states—isn't waiting on a global agreement blessed by Washington to invest in green technologies. With the ice caps melting up north, some worry that we might be heading toward a unipolar world. Thankfully, the global response to climate change looks distinctly multipolar. If acceleration toward a low-carbon world continues—bolstered by technological innovation and further US and Chinese steps toward carbon pricing—the world will avoid catastrophic climate change.

Too many environmentalists suggest that dealing with water shortages or other natural resource constraints and with climate change will take immediate and radical retooling of the global economy. It won't. Responses to these challenges are practical and affordable, costing about 2 percent of global GDP, or one year's worth of economic growth. If you give out the message that the only path to sustainability goes through dramatically lower standards of living, everyone else is put off—and especially people in developing countries. And once you've convinced yourself that the world is on an inevitable course to disaster if some corner of the US Midwest is fracked but once more, or India builds another car factory, then the only logical thing to do when the fracking or the building occurs is to sit back, put your TOMS-shod feet up on the couch, and drink microbrewed herbal tea until civilization collapses. Our global environmental challenges, however, aren't that dire—or at the least, they aren't that dire *yet*.

So if you're really just looking for a reason to strap on some THE END OF THE WORLD IS NIGH placards and go for a walk, better excuses probably remain the continued threat of global thermonuclear war or a rogue asteroid. The fight to move to a sustainable global growth path is one for the hard-nosed optimist. With bold but plausible and affordable action, the planet can enjoy continued global growth, convergence in living standards, and two billion more people, all while preserving the global commons.

But the question is: do we really want that? Chapter 6 discusses the continued attraction of turning our back on this planetary bounty — and why that is such a ridiculous idea.

CHAPTER SIX

The Folly of Fortress Thinking

T HERE IS A BIG SIGN ON one of the bridges over the Delaware River in Trenton, New Jersey: TRENTON MAKES, THE WORLD TAKES. It is a motto dating from 1911, when Trenton was a major manufacturing center. The city even made the world's largest-ever bathtub to fit the 350-pound President William Taft. But Trenton's manufacturing heyday is long in the past. And despite the growth of state government jobs, the city's population is down nearly one-third from its peak in 1950. Like most places in the United States, Trenton now relies on service industries for employment. The steel ropes, farm tools, mattresses, and watches that it used to manufacture are now mostly imported. Trenton doesn't make much at all anymore. Could we bring Trenton back to economic vitality by closing off trade, compelling us to make watches and farm tools in the United States again? Or if it is the growing Hispanic population in the city that is the problem, would stronger border controls help bring back Trenton?

For some, isolationism is a seemingly attractive way to respond to relative decline. The United States could stick another few thousand National Guard troops on the southern border, ramp up tariffs, put new quotas on goods, and pile on regulations and punitive taxation to stymie international financial flows. The US Transportation Security Administration could try to make the international flying experience still less pleasant than it already is. Then America wouldn't have to deal with a new, richer world—and maybe we'd even slow growth a little in the Rest as a side benefit.

Of course, more reasonable people have better-founded doubts about the benefits of openness in a world where money, goods, and people are increasingly mobile and where it seems that more and more of what America used to do best is now done better elsewhere. But the evidence that barriers to trade or overseas investment are the answer to the country's economic woes is threadbare. While US unemployment remained above 7 percent in 2013, excluding immigrants (documented or not) would do little or nothing to improve native-born job prospects. In fact, migrants (documented or not) are already a vital part of the nation's economy and are likely to become more so as the US population ages. More immigration control would slow economic growth, and isolationism would only work to speed America's drift toward the backwaters. The US economy is already deeply enmeshed with the rest of the world, and it will be increasingly reliant on cooperation with nouveau riche nations like Brazil and China to sustain quality-of-life improvements at home in areas from trade and finance to the environment. Outdated attitudes toward the developing world will only cost the United States trade and investment opportunities—as well as jobs.

Moreover, America's overreaction to the threats of undocumented migration and terrorism and to military challenges is placing an immense burden on the country's economy—not just directly through the bloated budgets of the Department of Homeland Security and the Pentagon, but indirectly through the chilling effect on tourism and business travel to the United States. Fortress policies slow integration, even though it is integration that is the surest path to increased national security.

The situation in Europe is much the same: while geography and history make the region less susceptible to the attractions of isolationism, the response to the recent economic crisis has been to turn inward. In 1995, 39 percent of people in Britain thought the number of immigrants coming to Britain should be reduced "a lot." By 2011 that had climbed to 51 percent—despite the fact that the long-term solution to Europe's problem is to expand links outward.

o o o

POLLS SUGGEST THAT the proportion of Americans who mention war, immigration, terrorism, or "other foreign affairs issues" as the most important problem facing the United States added up to 4 percent in August 2012. That was down from 14 percent in January 2010. These responses put all foreign affairs concerns together on an equal footing with the single answer "morality." After a decade of damaging overseas entanglements and global economic crisis, Americans just don't want to think about the rest of the world. But this is one of those cases where America's leaders might actually want to *lead,* because what is going on in the rest of the world has never been so important to Americans as it is today—especially when it comes to the issue that regularly tops polls as the most significant problem facing the United States: the economy.[1]

According to World Bank data, in constant dollars, US exports climbed from $161 billion to $1,531 billion between 1970 and 2010—nearly a tenfold increase—and now account for 13 percent of the nation's output. A total of 9.7 million US workers are employed by export industries, and the US Department of Commerce suggests that every billion dollars of exports support over five thousand US jobs.[2] Compare that year-in year-out impact to the 900,000 to 4.7 million jobs the Congressional Budget Office estimates were supported by the $800 billion American Recovery and Reinvestment Act (ARRA, aka "the stimulus bill") in 2010—the year of its biggest impact. Or the 200,000 to 1.2 million jobs the ARRA sustained in 2012.[3]

These export industry jobs rely on a strong global economy, of course—in fact, US exports to the nineteen countries worldwide that more than doubled the size of their economies over the past ten years increased about fivefold, to $119 billion. But export jobs also rely on easy trading relationships bolstered by international agreements that keep tariffs and quotas low, alongside efficient ports that don't gum up the flow of goods with bureaucratic security and customs procedures. And the imports that we have seen are increasingly important to preserving the quality of life of the median American require exactly the same efficient movement of goods.

When it comes to the flow of money, global financial integration measured as the stock of world financial liabilities to world GDP was between 20 and 30 percent in 1913; today it is closer to 200 percent. Of course, back in 1950 the United States alone accounted for about one-third of net exports of global capital. Today the United States and Europe borrow heavily from China, among others—the rest of the planet owns about one-third of US federal debt, for example.[4]

America and Europe both are also increasingly reliant on the flow of *people* to ensure that their economies thrive. If trade involves services—including growth sectors for US exporters like holidays and education and entertainment—like as not it also involves the efficient movement of employees. That cannot happen without a cheap, reliable, hassle-light airport infrastructure alongside immigration systems that don't make travel a nightmare worthy of Stephen King.

But more significantly, foreign-born workers are an increasing part of the backbone of Western economies. The global stock of migrants in 2000 was 165 million—up from 92 million in 1960. It has since increased to more than 200 million. Despite all of the vocal opposition to immigration, the share of foreign-born in the populations of high-income countries doubled between 1985 and 2005, reaching almost 9 percent. An increasing number of those immigrants were highly skilled, and the percentage who were college graduates increased fourfold between 1975 and 2000.[5]

In 2000 the United States remained the most important migrant destination in the world, according to World Bank research. America is home to one-fifth of the world's migrants and the top destination for migrants from sixty sending countries. A little over 6.3 percent of the US population are noncitizens, and another 5 percent are naturalized, according to the Census Bureau. And that's pretty much all that keeps the United States as still arguably the largest economy. If it wants to stay up near the top, it had better find some more people to come in.[6]

Not least, Americans need migrants to keep their retirement portfolios healthy. Carl Lin of Rutgers University looked at the impact on tech stock prices of a doubling in visas for skilled foreign workers in the United States thanks to the 1998 American Competitiveness and Workforce Improvement Act. High-tech industries absorb around 80 percent of the visa applicants. In fact, migrants account for over 60 percent of PhD software engineers and more than half of medical scientists in the United States. Lin estimates that in the month after the act passed, firms in the high-tech industries enjoyed 15 percent and higher cumulative excess returns—a measure of the impact of the news on stock prices.[7]

More broadly, a Kauffman Foundation study by researcher Vivek Wadhwa suggested that, in 2006, foreign nationals residing in the United States were named as inventors or co-inventors on one-quarter of all patent applications filed from the United States. Wadhwa's study of foreign-born entrepreneurs found that one-quarter of science and technology companies founded between 1995 and 2005 had a foreign-born lead technologist or chief economist. These firms employed 450,000 workers.[8]

Entrepreneurial migrants are a vital part of increasing gains from global trade and finance as well. Across countries, doubling the bilateral stock of migrants between two countries raises trade between them by 10 percent. A 2011 review of forty-eight studies looking at immigration and trade by the University of Amsterdam's Masood Gheasi and his colleagues concluded that a 10 percent increase in the number of immigrants can be expected to increase the volume of trade by 1.5 percent.[9] And if the number of skilled emigrants doubles in a recipient country, foreign direct investment in their country of origin climbs 25 percent.[10]

But it is not just at the level of entrepreneurs and inventors that immigration is playing an increasingly vital role in sustaining Americans' quality of life. Patricia Cortes of Boston University and Jessica Pan of the National University of Singapore report that foreign-educated nurses now account for 20 percent or more of all those taking the US licensure exam—up from 6 percent in the mid-1980s. The considerable proportion of those nurses who were educated in the Philippines ended up earning 4 percent more than the average nursing wage in 2010. Cortes and Pan suggest that the reason for the premium is "quality differences," which presents one more reason why Americans should get serious about the costs of the fortress mentality: when they get sick, they probably want to be treated by a Filipino nurse.[11]

When it comes to less-skilled migration, there's the concern that if rich countries are flooded with poor people, those countries will just become poor too. But that concern is based on a misunderstanding of what makes rich countries rich. We've seen that it isn't scarce labor that makes Americans wealthy. It is better-functioning institutions and networks that allow people with the same skills doing the same job (like working in a McDonald's restaurant) to get paid so much more here than in India or in Africa. That's why recent evidence suggests that unskilled immigration to the United States actually *increases* average domestic wages and employment.

In fact, even unskilled native workers—the most vulnerable to competition from unskilled migrants—suffer little from migration. Economists Gianmarco Ottaviano and Giovanni Peri produced a paper for the National Bureau of Economic Research suggesting that unskilled workers' income might be 2 percent lower than it would be were there no migrants in the country. And in a more recent paper, Ottaviano, Peri, and Greg Wright look across US industries and argue that the net effect of immigration has been to create *more* jobs for native workers, including low-skilled workers. That's in part because many immigrants take jobs that would otherwise be sent abroad. As a result, they create demand for goods and services—as well as profits for domestic companies—that would benefit firms in other countries if the migrants weren't in the United States. In turn, the sale of products and additional revenue create demand for more workers in America.[12]

But what about undocumented workers? There are about 11 million undocumented immigrants in the United States, according to the Pew Hispanic Center. A comparatively conservative analysis by Gordon Hanson at the National Bureau of Economic Statistics suggests that wages for unskilled natives (the most at risk from undocumented competition) may be as much as 9 percent lower owing to undocumented immigration. But his estimates are distinctly on the pessimistic side. And what happens when America turns its back on undocumented migrants is clear from recent events in Georgia. The state-level crackdown on undocumented farmworkers reduced the labor available. Meanwhile, the United Farm Workers' "Take Our Jobs" campaign, designed to encourage unemployed Americans to take jobs in agriculture, placed only seven workers in jobs in the first three months of 2010. According to *Wired* magazine, farmers are now turning to $50,000 robots designed by Harvest Automation to fill the gap. As an employment strategy for low-skilled native workers, it is perhaps fair to say that Georgia's law didn't work out quite as expected. But estimates suggest that it cost the state over $1 billion in lost revenues.[13]

And there isn't really a downside to letting in more migrants. First, they really don't suck the treasury dry. A study of welfare payments to immigrants in the European Union by Alan Barrett and Bertrand Maître of Dublin's Economic and Social Research Institute concludes that while immigrants do see slightly higher rates of poverty, across all kinds of welfare support "lower rates of receipt for immigrants relative to natives are more typical" in the nineteen countries for which they have data.[14]

And second, when it comes to social impacts, if anything, immigration *lowers* crime rates—this according to studies of metropolitan census and crime report data by Lesley Williams Reid and her colleagues at Georgia State University. Moreover, an analysis by Alpaslan Akay and his colleagues at Germany's Institute for the Study of Labor suggests that native-born people in areas with larger immigrant populations actually report higher subjective well-being—they say they are happier.[15]

Looking forward, migration will play an important role in staving off the final end of American global dominance. We have seen that in a converging world, population is economic power. As income per person equalizes across countries, relative economy size is determined more and more by the number of people in each country. The United Nations predicts that China's population will rise from 1,275 million in 2000 to 1,395 million at midcentury. The numbers for the United States are 285 million and 409 million—a far more rapid growth rate. America's population will climb from 22 percent of China's to 29 percent over the half-century. And about four-fifths of that US population growth will be due to new immigrants and their descendants. The relative position of the United States in the output rankings will be far stronger thanks to all of those extra people.[16]

But increasing migration will have some real benefits for native-born Americans beyond extending whatever psychological comfort comes from being near-top nation. As the baby boom generation retires, the need for immigrant labor to sustain rich-world lifestyles—gardeners, child care providers, restaurant workers, cleaners—will become greater. That problem used to look less serious in the United States than it did in Europe because, with a historical fertility rate near 2.1 compared to well below 2.0 in Europe, the demographic transition in America looked to be less dramatic. But since the financial crisis, US fertility has also dropped below two children born per woman. As the average age of Americans climbs over the next twenty years, the Census Bureau suggests that the number of people age sixty-five or over will increase from 22 to 35 percent of the working-age population. Add in kids, and that means every one hundred people of working age will be supporting eighty-three people above or below working age by 2030.

Just as worrying, an analysis by Moshe Hazan and Hosny Zoabi of Jerusalem's Hebrew University finds that an important reason for historically large families in the United States was cheap child care, much of it provided by undocumented workers. If low-skilled migration stops, the fertility rate could remain permanently depressed and the current long-term "crisis" in entitlement programs, from Medicare to Social Security, that rely on a good ratio of workers to retirees will become a considerably more urgent problem. And with fewer people to teach children their ABCs or collect the oldsters' greens fees, prices will rise. Want to keep the cost of living down? Bring in some cheap labor from abroad.[17]

The story is similar—if not worse—in Europe. In 1960, again according to World Bank data, a little over one in ten of the British population were above the age of sixty-five, while around one-quarter were below the age of fifteen. Today those figures are about equal, at 17 percent. The numbers are broadly the same across the continent. By 2030, Europe will be increasingly desperate for young workers—and lamenting the anti-immigrant policies instituted during the second decade of the new century.[18]

o   o   o

BECAUSE THE WEST'S TREATMENT of visitors and migrants alike gets worse and worse, there was much discussion a few years back over the fact that the average cow in the West got a considerably bigger government transfer than the average person in Africa got in Western aid. But that debate missed a big part of the story. It isn't just *domestic* cows that get better treatment than do foreign humans; *foreign* cows get treated better than foreign humans too.

In fact, cows are overrunning America's borders with the complicity of the US government. There are no caps on the number of cattle allowed in each year, and permanent bovine immigration into the United States has dwarfed human immigration of late. Two million cattle entered the country in 2009, according to the US Department of Agriculture. Only a little over one million human immigrants became permanent residents in 2009, while the undocumented immigrant population actually fell that year. That suggests the net flow of humans was about one-tenth the inflow of cattle.

And if you think you were treated as cattle by the immigration and customs authorities on your last trip, you live in a dream world. Cows can travel across global borders with relative impunity—covered by the umbrella of the World Trade Organization (WTO) and the North America Free Trade Agreement (NAFTA). When violence in Mexico made it more dangerous for US government officials to travel across the border to pre-process bovine immigrants, the US Department of Agriculture immediately responded by opening up additional facilities inside the United States to ensure that the relocation of the cows wasn't delayed.

And the benefits of being bovine don't stop at the border. Once in the United States, Canadian or Mexican cattle have to be treated just as a native-born cow and can't be labeled differently. Canadian *people* have no such luck. One implication of this favoritism is that cows get immediate access to the US welfare system. The nine million US dairy cows alone got $1.35 billion in subsidies in 2009. Per bovine household (aka herd, which averages around 133 cows), that's about $20,000 a year. And pretty much every dairy cow is a welfare queen, native and immigrant alike.[19] Meanwhile, annual payments for the average *human* household on welfare are only around $16,800—and of course, the great majority of immigrants aren't on welfare at all, while undocumented and nonpermanent human residents aren't even eligible.[20]

At first glance, then, it might appear to be good news that some in the US government are seeking closer bovine-human equality in treatment. Sadly, it looks as though the attempts are toward equality at the lowest common denominator. Congressman Steve King noted about his proposal to put an electric fence between the US and Mexico to stop human immigrants, "we do this with livestock all the time."[21] In the same vein, federal authorities have started attaching radio-frequency ID tags like those used on livestock to students from India.

o   o   o

SIMILARLY, THE IMMENSE overreaction to the security threat presented by terrorists is making travel considerably more harrowing for citizens and visitors alike. Out of the 150,000 murders in the United States between September 12, 2001, and the end of 2010, Islamic terrorism accounted for fewer than three dozen. It is true that domestic right-wing extremist groups are a bigger danger—they have carried out twice as many attacks as jihadist-affiliated groups in the United States since 9/11. But both domestic and foreign terrorism pose just a minor threat to Americans.[22]

The US State Department used to publish annual statistics on the global number of people killed each year by acts of international terrorism. The *global* total for the five years from 1999 to 2003—spanning the 9/11 attacks on New York and Washington—was 5,535 people. Those deaths were a tragedy, but it is worth putting them in perspective. They amount to less than one-fifth of the number of people who died in traffic fatalities in the United States in 2010 alone (which, by the way, saw the lowest level of traffic deaths in sixty-one years thanks to improved auto safety). In fact, extremist Islamic terrorism results in 200 to 400 deaths *worldwide* outside of the war zones of Afghanistan and Iraq—the same number, notes John Mueller of Ohio State University, as die in bathtubs in the United States alone each year.[23]

And yet, not a single Tub Security Agency employee scans our rubber duckies before allowing them to enter the bathroom, while the other TSA (Transportation Security Administration) has a budget of nearly $8 billion. That's why this TSA is left with too many officers and not enough to do. The agency's "Top 10 Good Catches of 2011," as reported on its blog, did include 1,200 firearms and—the TSA's number-one find—some C4 explosives (sadly, only found on the return flight).[24] But not a single terrorist was unmasked, notes Bruce Schneier. And those "Top 10 Good Catches" should be put in the context of the longer list of confiscations, which included the four-inch-long plastic rifle on a GI Joe action doll ("it's a replica") and a light saber.[25]

When combined with enhanced security related to immigration—questionable innovations like face-to-face interviews for even short-term visas, which give more discretion to often-capricious immigration officials with no evidence of increased security—the fortress mentality represented by the US Department of Homeland Security has cost not only lives, thanks to incentivizing people to travel by (dangerous) car rather than (safer) airplane, but considerable treasure.

Over the long term, anything that reduces the desire or ability of tourists and businesspeople to travel to the United States reduces revenues for hotels, restaurants, and entertainment venues. The United States earned $150 billion from foreign visitors in 2011, but the US share of international tourist numbers has fallen from 17 percent to 12 percent since 2000—not least because of the increasingly byzantine process involved in getting a visa to the country. And fewer travelers leads to less trade and investment, as we've seen.[26]

But ignore these costs and just look at the price of fortress upkeep. According to one estimate of the direct and indirect costs borne by the United States as a result of 9/11, the *New York Times* suggests that the attacks have caused $55 billion in "toll and physical damage," that the economic impact has been $123 billion, and that costs related to increased homeland security spending and funding wars have totaled $3,105 billion.[27] Mueller and Stewart estimate that the government's spending on homeland security over the period 2002 to 2011 accounted for around $580 billion of that total.[28] Federal immigration enforcement cost $18 billion in 2012 alone—considerably more than was spent on all other major federal law enforcement agencies, including the Federal Bureau of Investigation (FBI) and the Bureau of Alcohol, Tobacco, and Firearms (ATF), combined.[29]

And then, of course, there is all of the military expenditure. On that count, the United States isn't doing as badly as previous superpowers. As Tufts's Michael Beckley points out, "Past hegemons succumbed to imperial overstretch after fighting multifront wars against major powers and spending more than 10 percent of their GDPs on defense. The United States, by contrast, spends 4 percent of its GDP on defense."[30]

But, as the 2012 movie *Red Dawn* suggests, it makes little sense that America has its largest military budget ever. *Red Dawn* is a remake of the 1984 film of the same name in which a bunch of teenagers led by Patrick Swayze fight off an invading Soviet army in Colorado. The original never achieved quite the critical acclaim of *Dirty Dancing*, but it has been viewed as a work of staggering beauty and intelligence compared to the remake—not least because the country that manages to invade the United States only to be battled by a misfit band of kids in that remake is North Korea. That would be the famine-ridden country whose invasion forces probably really could be defeated by a bunch of video-game-addled US teens.

Apparently the movie was originally going to star the Chinese as the bad guys, which would have made a little more sense—but also doomed sales prospects in a growing export market for Hollywood. Still, as we've seen, China just isn't a plausible military adversary for the United States today—or anytime soon either.

In short, the problem for Hollywood when it comes to US invasion movies is that it is more plausible to imagine the enemy forces arriving from outer space than from Russia or Japan or China or (especially) North Korea. That tells you something about how secure the country is. The US military retains vital roles in the fight against global terror, protecting sea-lanes from piracy and supporting humanitarian missions. But it is surely questionable that these tasks require the same base defense budget that we had in 1985 (and that leaves out the costs of Afghanistan and Iraq). The mid-1980s saw the height of the Cold War and the summit of President Reagan's defense budget increases; it was a time when US and Soviet troops massed across Central Europe and global thermonuclear war was an ever-present risk.

And it isn't just America experiencing relative serenity, but also the country's closest allies across the Atlantic. Before today, the last time the Rhine hadn't been crossed by armies with hostile intent for so long was more than two thousand years ago, according to economic historian Brad de Long.[31] And globally, we've seen that wars between nation-states have been incredibly rare since 1945. With the decline of the Cold War and the growing legitimacy of new states, even civil wars have waned.

A recent YouGov poll suggested that Americans are well aware of where global influence comes from these days. Asked which single factor matters most to that influence—cultural attractiveness, the economy, or military strength—only 26 percent said that a country's military strength is most important, while 45 percent said that it's the size of the economy. And economic strength is increasingly reliant on pacific foreign policies.[32]

Governments recognize this too. Despite the rhetoric and expenditure around conducting a war on terror at home and abroad—and while the record of the FBI, not to mention the New York Police Department, had hardly been spotless when it came to a domestic response—the Bush administration followed the 9/11 terror attack with a sincere effort to reach out to American Muslims, rather than locking them up, as the federal government had done with Japanese Americans during World War II. Trade and migration continued unabated. As columnist Dan Gardner has noted recently, "The simple truth is that 10 years after 9/11, every nation in the Western world is more culturally diverse and pluralistic than ever."[33] That was the brave and right response, of course, but it is time to implement it more fully—to swap out the portcullis for the welcome mat.

○ ○ ○

AS BEFITS A GROUP OF NATIONS that long ago gave up on individual global power status, European states suffer somewhat less from the fortress mentality. They trade more, invest more, and send more of their students and businesspeople abroad. Survey evidence suggests that they better recognize the importance of the Rest to their well-being. That said, fortress thinking around immigration in particular remains common in Europe—indeed, in many countries it is far more virulent and misinformed than in the United States, sustaining neo-Nazi parties that get elected to seats in parliament. According to a 2010 German Marshall Fund survey, only a little more than one-third of Americans think that there are currently "too many" immigrants in the country. That compares to 59 percent in Britain. This despite the fact that, just as in the United States, migrants play a vital role in European economies, and demographic trends suggest that role will rapidly expand.[34]

So if many people in both Europe and America are wrong to think foreign competition or immigrants are taking their jobs, who is? One answer to that is to look at who is employing fewer people than they used to. Between the start of 2009 and early 2013, private-sector payrolls in the United States rose by two million, while public-sector payrolls went *down* by over 700,000. At least over the last few years in the United States, the answer to the question "Who's responsible for the jobs crisis?" is "The government." And the government is responsible not only directly by sacking people, but indirectly by skimping on the retraining programs, infrastructure, and support for innovation that are necessary to create new job opportunities in a rapidly changing global economy. In Europe, too, it is the government that is responsible for the jobs crisis: when European countries imposed austerity measures in the middle of a recession, the result, unsurprisingly, was falling demand and falling job rolls along with it. Americans and Europeans should be thankful that at least the rest of the world continued to grow, demanding goods and services and buying government debt on international markets, while the West wallowed in a self-created recession.

Because the international economic environment matters more to the West than ever before, so do international institutions of all sorts—from the Basel Accords on bank regulation to agreements on climate, to global regulation of medicines, to cooperation on fish stocks, to shared intelligence on international crime. The United Nations, without a single black helicopter to call its own, would surely lose in a battle against a Texas militia—or even against a ragtag group of American teens intent on defending the homeland—but that doesn't mean international institutions are irrelevant to US or European national security.

The role of such institutions is discussed in Chapter 8. But before we discuss the national and international policies that would enable the West to benefit from the rise of the Rest, it is worth looking at the meaning of global economic transformation for individual Americans and Europeans, and the positive benefits it can have if Western governments help them embrace those opportunities.

CHAPTER SEVEN

Global Nomads

EVEN THOSE AMERICANS and Europeans who stay an-chored to the West from birth to death can enjoy huge opportunities from a world made wealthier through trade, finance, the spread of ideas, and the migration of people. But the real spoils of the rise of the Rest will go to Westerners who are willing to get on an international flight once in a while.

At the moment, only one in five eighteen- to twenty-four-year-olds in the United States even has a passport.[1] US under-graduates accounted for just 0.4 percent of the global total of students enrolled in college outside their country of citizenship in 2011. Data from the Institute for International Education sug-gest that only about 0.06 percent of US students enrolled in a full-time undergraduate degree program are overseas (and al-most half of them only got as far as the United Kingdom).[2]

And after college, the data on US expatriates suggest, the United States has less than one-third the number of high-skilled emigrants as the United Kingdom (despite a population five times as large) and half as many as Germany.³ More broadly, the United States has never seen anything on the scale of recent European migration to nouveau riche nations like Chile and Angola. Around 30,000 Spaniards moved to Argentina from June 2009 to November 2010. And the number of Portuguese employed in Angola almost quintupled, growing to 100,000, from 2003 to 2011. In terms of relative population, that would be the same as three million Americans shipping off to the country's ex-colony, the Philippines, in search of a better life.⁴

In part that's because most Americans reckon they live in El Dorado right now—they're in the promised land over the sea already. And certainly, average US standards of living remain notably higher than in the Rest and will do so for some time. Despite the reverse-migration, the same is true for Europe.

Nonetheless, there are considerable opportunities for a better life when some of it is lived elsewhere, and even comparatively isolated Americans are already getting out more. From 1996 to 2009, the number of US citizens traveling just to Africa tripled, to 399,000 a year. Also, 260,000 US students studied abroad in the 2008–2009 academic year, up from around 75,000 twenty years earlier.

And that may be a sign of things to come—young Americans increasingly recognize the huge opportunities presented by traveling, studying, and working abroad. More than half of college students are considering study abroad, and 30 percent of those considering the option think that such study "is the start to my international career." Kids are just more cosmopolitan these days.⁵

That's great news for those adventurous students—and great news for the people who stay back at home. As the rest of the world gets richer, healthier, more stable, and more democratic, the options when it comes to places to learn, to make money, and to make a life have never been broader. A growing band of global nomads will live in many countries—and truck and barter with many more—over the course of a lifetime. They will benefit from higher-quality and lower-cost care and education services, alongside more varied and more remunerative ways to make a living. And if seizing those opportunities is good for the individual adventurer, it also strengthens ties across countries, creating more global trade, investment, and innovation, and that is great for everyone.

o   o   o

START WITH THE educational opportunities. The College Board suggests that more than two-fifths of full-time undergraduate students attend a college that charges less than $9,000 per year for tuition and fees, but that, at the other end, more than one-quarter are in a school that charges $36,000 or more. Some of those students get scholarships, and many get federal aid—but plenty don't, or they don't get enough. A recent Pew Research Center analysis suggests that 57 percent of Americans think college is only fair or poor value for the money. And three-quarters argue that college is too expensive for most Americans to afford.[6]

There is a simple answer to such concerns: shop around for a better deal. If Junior is willing to travel a little bit farther—to a college overseas—the world offers some incredible bargains for quality tertiary education, with the option of free language and cultural immersion thrown in. Tuition costs for foreign students at some of the best universities in Asia, Europe, and Africa can be as low as $4,000—well below half of the median cost in the United States. And some are providing an education that is the equal of well-known schools in America and Europe.

Global university rankings, like those from Shanghai University, the UK *Times Higher Education Supplement,* and Quacquarelli Symonds, are hardly free of controversy, and they are rarely centered on the student experience—they take into account things like the number of Nobel Prizes awarded to faculty, or how many citations the average professor receives in journal articles that are read by a global audience of forty-three on a good day. Nonetheless, these rankings provide a broad measure of the potential for excellence in learning.[7]

The rankings suggest that the United States remains top dog in terms of world-beating universities. Seven out of the top ten in the *Times* ranking are American schools, for example. At the same time, all three rankings have at least two UK universities among the top ten, and the Quacquarelli Symonds ranking helpfully reports that the UK universities at the top charge foreign students around $22,000 in annual tuition—compared to domestic fees of around $38,000 for the top US schools.

Ninety-nine percent of US and European college applicants surely doubt their chances at Harvard and MIT, or have little hope of spending three years shivering in the windswept fens of Cambridge or the fog-bound damp of Oxford. The good news for those people is that the opportunities for bargains get better as you go down the rankings: McGill in Canada is ahead of Duke in the United States, for example, and charges about half as much in fees. And the Shanghai top five hundred include about thirty-seven universities from low- and middle-income economies. Institutions like the University of São Paulo in Brazil and Fudan University in China rank above renowned American educational establishments like George Washington University in Washington, DC, or Notre Dame.

For the cost-conscious consumer of tertiary education, this high quality comes at a truly bargain basement price.

South Africa's University of Cape Town beats out Georgetown University on the Quacquarelli Symonds rankings, but Georgetown's fees are $40,000-plus, compared to an upper end of $8,000 for foreign students attending Cape Town. And only one of the two universities comes with quality local wine and views of Table Mountain. Or what about the Indian Institute of Technology in Delhi? Ranked a little above Notre Dame in the Quacquarelli Symonds rankings, its annual fees are somewhere between one-fifth and one-seventh of the price of Notre Dame.

Want to combine a quality education with language immersion? Peking University—forty-ninth by the *Times* criteria, above Penn State—charges between $4,000 and $6,000 in tuition a year. Or for those wanting to brush up their Spanish, the Catholic University of Chile ranks considerably above Wake Forest, but the fees are 80 percent lower.

The even better news is that many developing-country universities score better on the teaching environment than they do on overall rankings. For example, the *Times* scores suggest that Peking University's ranking on teaching is better than that of all but fifteen of the forty-nine universities above it on the *Times* list. And a growing number of foreign students are benefiting from cheap, quality education by flocking to universities in middle-income countries. In 2009, three developing economies—Russia, China, and South Africa—attracted nearly 250,000 overseas students among them, according to the OECD. Americans—and Europeans—should be joining the rush while they can still get in.[8]

o o o

AS WE HAVE SEEN with trade in goods, trade in services like education is not just about value, it is also about choice. Students who go abroad to study can experience very different teaching styles in different subjects taught in different languages and locales. Similarly, once they've graduated, some of those students may take advantage of exciting job opportunities in developing countries that would be unlike anything they could do back home.

Not least, perhaps because stars from Bono to Angelina Jolie have made it cool to care about global poverty, working in international development is hot. The website GradSchools.com lists 199 master's programs in international development meant to prepare students for providing technical assistance to local water and sanitation departments or dealing with the logistics of emergency food programs. DevEx, the international development portal, says that employers working in the aid arena can search through its database of 400,000 candidates. And the World Bank's Young Professionals Program—a route to a permanent position at the organization—routinely attracts more than 10,000 applicants for about thirty spots each year.[9]

The global development industry is one way to contribute to a better world. Sure, a lot of money spent in aid programs or by charities is wasted. Think of the release of 10,000 pink balloons in Kabul in order to create "a living sculpture that brought about joy, wonderment and a new sense of awareness to people," or the earlier parachute drop of 2.4 million PopTarts across Afghanistan—to say nothing of the failed energy projects costing hundreds of millions of dollars that may never deliver power. But working for an organization like UNICEF or the Gates Foundation to increase global access to new vaccines and basic medical care is one of the most effective ways ever to save lives.

But in the economies of the dynamic Rest, there are a lot of other opportunities for exciting (and lucrative) employment beyond the aid industry, of course. Developing countries now contain a number of innovative, world-beating companies to work for, like ZTE, Baidu, or Tata. And in a world where foreign direct investment in Africa was worth more than aid over the last decade—above $60 billion in 2010 alone—hopefully more young, idealistic graduate students will go into the private sector of countries from South Africa to Ethiopia to work in firms that are making a real difference to the quality of life in poor countries—and perhaps even help them make more of a difference.[10]

Want to help continue the mobile phone revolution in developing countries, for example? A number of international companies provide subscriptions to 5.6 billion customers worldwide. Vodafone employs nearly 84,000 people and provides telecom services to 214 million subscribers in developing countries. Access to telephones provided by companies like Vodafone is associated with all sorts of good things: improving the prices that farmers and fishermen can get for their output and increasing employment in rural South Africa by as much as 15 percent, for example. And with 14 million customers in Kenya in 2011—more than one-third of the total population—Vodafone's M-Pesa mobile banking service has had a huge impact on access to financial services in a country with fewer than 900 bank branches (about one branch for every 46,000 people).[11]

Or what about improving access to personal hygiene and preventing deaths from diseases like diarrhea? Unilever products were sold to more than two billion consumers in 180 countries worldwide in 2010, 53 percent of the company's revenues came from developing markets, and 97,000 of the company's employees were in Africa, Asia, and Central and Eastern Europe. In India, where

Unilever's Lifebuoy soap has the largest market share, the firm ran an 18,000-village campaign that used a range of marketing techniques, from setting up health clubs, to supporting school plays, to encouraging people to wash their hands with soap. This is a real case of doing good by doing well. A review of evidence in the medical journal *The Lancet* suggests that washing one's hands with soap is associated with at least a 40 percent decline in the risk of diarrhea, and that if everyone worldwide washed their hands using soap after going to the bathroom and before preparing food, between 500,000 and 1.4 million lives would be saved each year. (Although it should be noted that the study was financed by Unilever itself.)[12]

Of course, the private sector is motivated first and foremost by profits, not the drive to promote sustainable development. The name of the chemical company Union Carbide will forever be associated with the 1984 gas leak from its chemical plant in Bhopal, India, which killed thousands. And the German company Siemens recently paid $1.6 billion in fines as punishment for bribes it made around the world. But historically, well-regulated commerce has been the driving force for poverty reduction and economic growth worldwide. Working for a law-abiding private firm that is creating jobs for poor people and products for everyone is one of the most effective methods to increase the impact of that commerce. It is also a way to make a lot of money and lead a globe-spanning life.

o o o

RELATED TO THAT, fast-growing economies are also a great place for Americans to put their investments. Morgan Stanley's emerging market stock index has outperformed the S&P 500 by about 4 percent a year over the past decade. There is also a range of attractive investment opportunities for US firms and entre-preneurs—think Starbucks and Yum! Brands. In short, a richer world makes for a richer America.

Moreover, for successful entrepreneurs and investors, select cities in developing regions are becoming very pleasant places to live. According to the Knight Frank survey of wealth and prop-erty advisers to "high-net-worth" individuals (worth $100 mil-lion–plus), the obscenely rich still predominantly like Western cities. Asked to judge which cities were the most important to their clients, they put London, New York, Hong Kong, Paris, Singapore, Miami, Geneva, Shanghai, Beijing, and Berlin on their top-ten list—that's six out of ten for the West. But asked to forecast ten years forward, the advisers suggested that, while London and New York will still be at the top, Miami will have been replaced by São Paulo on the list.[13] In other words, in a world where half of all $100 million–plus individuals already live in Asia, Africa, Eastern Europe, or Latin America, half of the top-ten favorite cities of the obscenely rich will soon be located in those same regions.

Even those who are only in the global top 10 percent of in-comes (which includes most people in the West) can some times afford a quality of life in many developing countries that can be considerably higher than back home. For all of its growth, the Rest remains poorer than the West, and as a result, anything that requires a lot of time and personal attention—restaurants, clean-ing services, day care, elder care—is comparably cheap. So if you have kids, or if you need help getting out of bed, or if you can't cook, there can be real advantages to moving east or south, at least for a time. As these places get richer, personal services will become more expensive. But until global incomes come close to converging—and that is many decades away at best—the quality of services for the money is likely to be higher in many parts of the developing world.

There are particularly large opportunities presented by the nouveau riche world to the West's growing army of the sick and infirm. For the average American under age sixty-five (and they are not the expensive ones), health care expenditures added up to $4,255 a head in 2010, according to the Health Care Cost Institute. The figure for individuals between the ages of fifty-five and sixty-four was $8,327. The really expensive stuff involves inpatient care, which cost an average of $14,662 per person (inpatient surgical care reached an average of $27,000).[14] A partial answer to the family (and fiscal) burden of health care is to outsource it. Let people travel overseas to get health care at lower costs. They can throw in a holiday while they're abroad, and federal and state governments can save some cash too.

Medical tourism is already a big business. Bumrungrad Hospital in Bangkok sees tens of thousands of American patients each year, for example—part of an industry that brought 126,000 foreigners to Thailand for treatment in 2002. US patients are attracted not just by the low costs (appendectomy for $3,653, anyone?), but by the quality of treatment. Bumrungrad Hospital has international accreditation from the Joint Commission International—the global arm of the Joint Commission on Accreditation of Health Care Organizations, which is a leading certifying organization for US hospitals. And it isn't just Bumrungrad or Thailand: India's Apollo hospital chain has a 99 percent success rate in the 50,000-plus cardiac surgeries it has done—equal to the performance of the best US cardiac surgery centers.[15]

If you are still afraid of the quality of care provided by foreign doctors, it is no use staying at home anyway. As we have seen, a

lot of medical treatment in the United States is provided by migrants. According to Aaditya Mattoo and Randeep Rathindran
of the World Bank, there is a 25 percent chance that the physician
you visit in a US hospital was educated abroad—and the great
majority of those foreign-educated doctors come from developing countries. Your decision about where to seek medical care is
not really about the quality of the doctor who will treat you, but
about where you will be treated.[16]

Despite care of similar quality between the best foreign hospitals and US hospitals, the savings from medical tourism over
US costs can be considerable. Mattoo and Rathindran calculate
that knee surgery that costs over $10,000 in the United States
would cost only $1,500 in the best hospitals in India and Hun-
gary, including travel expenses. In the United States, 400,000
such procedures are performed each year—outsource one-quarter of them and that's an $850 million annual saving just for that
one procedure.

There are potential savings for Europeans when it comes to
medical treatment as well. But in countries with free national health
care, the incentives for individuals to save money on treatment by
going abroad are considerably reduced. The same does not always
apply to elder care, however, and increasingly Europeans are retiring elsewhere in Europe or even farther afield. Northern Europeans have a long tradition of retiring further south—in Provence
or the Costa del Sol, for instance. More recently, Germany has
seen many elderly citizens who need long-term care moving to
countries in Eastern Europe or even to Thailand. There are obvious downsides to importing elder care services—not least, distance
from family and friends. But for some people the trade-off—better
weather, better service, and a considerably reduced cost of care—
will be well worth it.

o o o

FOR MOST WESTERNERS for most of the time, it probably makes sense to stay put in a region that, on average, has the highest quality of life of anywhere in the world. But for a growing minority, it makes sense to spend a lot of time abroad—and for nearly everyone it makes sense to spend at least some more time overseas. So Westerners shouldn't just visit some of the more than 500 UNESCO World Heritage Sites, out of 962 in total, that are outside of Europe and North America. They should also study, volunteer, work, invest, convalesce, and retire overseas on occasion. They'll live a richer, more enjoyable life for it.

This argument may appear to sit ill with the contention in Chapter 4 that the West will gain from a growing Rest in part because the West will *export* services, including health and education, to Asian, African, and Latin American students and patients—and that immigration *into* the West will be a powerful source of the region's future prosperity. But just like the gains in growing trade from goods, the gains from growing trade in people can make both sides better off.

As long as immigration policies ensure that they can continue to attract many of the world's top students, the United States and Europe will doubtless retain most top spots in global university rankings for some time to come, for example. The benefits from having gotten good at educating early on are clear from the top-ten cases of Harvard (founded early enough to offer Galileo a visiting lectureship, in the apocryphal account), Cambridge (founded in 1209), and Oxford (founded three hundred–odd years before that). Being a place that produces brilliant graduates makes it easier to hire them to teach and do research—which helps guarantee another generation of excellent students. So in a growing global trade in education, in spite of its declining youth populations, the West is likely to remain a net exporter of educational services.

But the choices and opportunities presented to American and European students by global options in college education are immense—and by making possible more educational investment for less money, they offer less college debt and higher earnings. A similar logic applies to trade in health care services—the West should be both importing and exporting more of these services. Added to that, closer links through migration strengthen trade and investment ties and foster the transmission of ideas and norms, as we have seen. All of that is to the benefit of both the West and the Rest.

So just as it makes sense for the United States and Europe to foster both inward and outward investment at the same time, it is also a sensible policy for the West not only to encourage more students to come and study here—and then stay—but also to encourage Western youth to study and work in the Rest. Such policies are the subject of the next chapter.

CHAPTER EIGHT

Policies at Home to Gain from Abroad

REFLECTING THAT AMERICANS don't travel, study, or work abroad as much as their European counterparts, and despite the fact that America is dependent on the rest of the world more than ever, the country is still one of the least globally integrated. While US exports have been climbing, for example, 140 economies out of the 146 with export data from the World Bank in 2010 exported more than the United States as a share of their GDP. Only Nepal, Brazil, Haiti, Ethiopia, and Tonga did worse than the US export share of 13 percent of output. Even Afghanistan outdid the United States by 2 percent of GDP. China's export share was more than twice as big, at 30 percent.

Or look at investment trends. According to World Bank data, in 2010 US net outflows of foreign direct investment—where American investors were taking a 10 percent or larger share of a foreign company—amounted to 2.4 percent of US GDP. Twenty economies were above the United States in that share—compare Germany at 3.3 percent of GDP, Chile at 4.1 percent, or Singapore at 9.5 percent, for example.[1]

In a world where the Rest has the most dynamic economies and a growing share of total output, the West needs policies that will increase trade, investment, and the flow of people in both directions with those economies. Trade policies should back a dynamic relationship, not prop up declining US industries or domestic monopolies, though governments do have an important role to play in ensuring that displaced workers find new jobs. One tool for that will be expanding inward investment—rather than deterring it through protectionism wrapped up as "security concerns." Most importantly, the United States and the West as a whole must open up to immigration while there is still widespread desire to come, as well as encourage more out-migration to strengthen economic ties around the planet. Abandoning the fortress mentality in favor of open partnership is a matter of priority—because if the West doesn't do so on its terms today, it will likely have to do so on less favorable terms tomorrow.

o o o

IN 2012, RUSSIA JOINED the World Trade Organization, the global trade body that has slashed tariffs and quotas across the globe over rounds of negotiation dating back to the 1940s. Every year the proportion of world trade that takes place under the organization's rules climbs closer to 100 percent. And thanks to the WTO, the worldwide battle against trade tariffs has been almost completely won. Now the fight is over antiquated rules that hinder supply chain production that takes place across a number of countries (like iPad manufacture), limit the travel of people involved in trade, and stop firms from producing the same product for multiple markets without hundreds of design and packaging tweaks. Negotiators at the WTO in Geneva are well aware of these issues of trade facilitation, which increasingly occupy their time when they are given the power to discuss them by home-country governments actually interested in making a deal.

But a World Trade Organization round that could reduce such barriers across the planet has been stalled for a decade by disagreements over issues such as agricultural subsidies and intellectual property. Instead, the United States and Europe have retreated to using trade deals with small groups of countries and with each other because they no longer have the muscle to get everything they want in a global deal. And the bilateral deals often involve shortsighted attempts to *lower* the quality of regulation overseas. Further reducing their limited value is the fact that the agreements are larded with special-interest provisions. Recent US bilateral trade deals, for example, are trying to protect the wrong domestic industries (gas-guzzling autos, tobacco, and arms), using the wrong approaches (limits on health warnings and fuel efficiency standards in our treaty partners) under the wrong overall approach (bilateralism when we should be strengthening multilateralism). All for a few thousand unsustainable jobs at best—and a long-term impact that will reduce the competitiveness of America.

Take the tobacco conditions. Roughly one-third of the world's adult population smokes, and every year more than five million people die from it—more than from AIDS, tuberculosis, and malaria combined. But over the past thirty years, American trade negotiators have played an important role in levering open markets to US cigarette companies, which in turn use the same marketing tactics to addict a whole new generation of global smokers that worked so well back home before they were banned. Nearly every US trade and investment agreement over the past ten years reduced tobacco tariffs and facilitated the establishment of US-owned cigarette factories overseas, according to Thomas Bollyky of the Council on Foreign Relations.[2]

You might see that as "leveling the playing field" between domestic and imported nicotine, but given that 90 percent of the world lives in countries with low retail tax rates on cigarettes and limited or no marketing restrictions on tobacco, it is no surprise that these trade reforms have led to rapidly climbing smoking rates. Given that health is an input to productivity and we want developing markets to grow, expanding cancer rates in developing countries might be seen as a shortsighted strategy.

More broadly, it is in the interests of America to set the precedent that trade and trade deals are in the interest of the Rest. The United States needs access to these markets in the future, when they will be in a stronger bargaining position. After all, the US and EU share of trade fell from 31 to 20 percent over the first decade of the twenty-first century alone. It might be best if developing countries' memories of past trade deals with the West did not involve enforced deregulation of carcinogens.

The extent to which fortress thinking has dominated thinking about trade is also clear from the fact that an assistant secretary at the Department of Homeland Security in charge of immigration and customs enforcement went all the way to a Walt Disney sound stage in Hollywood recently to announce a crackdown on global piracy. He declared that "the reason the Department of Homeland Security is protecting Shrek is because we are all about protecting the homeland. We're all about protecting American interests." Doubtless the Facebook page of Shrek nemesis Lord Farquaad is already downloaded on the National Security Agency servers.[3]

The United States is now pushing other countries to adopt an intellectual property regime that is harmful to the US domestic economy, will be more harmful to its trade partners, and is significantly against America's own long-term interests in favor of the flow of technologies across borders in a world where most innovation occurs overseas.

As a result of pressure from US technology firms and "creative industries" such as Disney, the 1994 agreement signed in Marrakesh that established the World Trade Organization involved significant intellectual property provisions covering copyrights, patents, and trademarks. Average copyright and patent protection periods in developing countries increased from four to seven years prior to the agreement to a minimum of twenty years after it came into force.[4]

And now, with the active support of the Motion Picture Association of America (MPAA), US bilateral trade agreements are adding as much as twenty years to copyright terms above World Trade Organization rules. Not least, the US agreements with South Korea, Peru, and Colombia, all signed in the last few years, stipulated that these countries toughen their intellectual property restrictions. The Central American and Caribbean trade agreements also included provisions for longer copyright and trademark protection.

The reason the US "creative industries" are interested in stronger intellectual property restrictions worldwide is obvious: it allows them to go on making money even if they're not creative anymore. Of course Disney wants longer copyright protection on Mickey Mouse—all the actual work of creating him happened seventy-five years ago, so whatever Disney gets in license and usage payments is free money. And as we've seen, overseas markets are an increasingly important source of income for studios churning out clunkers like *Battleship*. They might make even more money with stronger, longer global monopoly enforcement.

But the MPAA gamely argues that extended knowledge monopolies are in the public interest—that they are good for both US and developing-country economic growth and security. The lobby group paid for a Rand study titled *Film Piracy, Organized Crime, and Terrorism,* which suggested that "terrorist groups have used the proceeds of film piracy to finance their activities" and argued for stronger intellectual property restrictions to counter that. Another MPAA report even made the case that stronger restrictions are essential to global broadband rollout.[5]

The evidence just doesn't support such claims. While reasonable intellectual property regimes help foster creativity and are a growing and important source of export revenue, what is good for Scrooge McDuck isn't necessarily good for the United States or the world.

It is complicated to make a true accounting of the net impact of current copyright and trademark infringement. A recent survey of the academic literature on the impact of piracy concluded that "results diverge considerably even for the relatively narrow question of whether file-sharing harms right-holders to musical works." But the survey finds that consumer benefits clearly and substantially outweigh whatever producer losses result from piracy. That suggests that some level of piracy is *good* for the economy at the current inflated levels of intellectual property protection.[6]

Regardless, these estimates are based on *infringement of current rules,* not on ever-longer extensions of knowledge monopolies in the first place, where the evidence in favor is even less compelling. Again, *some* level of monopoly protection for ideas is a useful way to stimulate creativity and will be a growing part of the West's export revenues. But the evidence in favor of extended copyright term lengths—from the 14 years granted by the world's first copyright law, the Statute of Anne, to 120 years under US current law—is weak at best. Apparently the original term was enough to provide incentive to Daniel Defoe to write *Robinson Crusoe* and to Jonathan Swift to write *Gulliver's Travels*—even if it may have taken the longer copyright terms of the modern day to encourage Snooki to write her debut novel, *A Shore Thing*. And twenty-year patent terms—one-sixth the length of copyrights—appear generous enough to have created a fairly robust stream of new inventions in the past.

Knowledge is a public good—and unlike common land, which is always at threat of overgrazing, there's no risk of tragic over-utilization of an idea ("play him off, keyboard cat" aside). Copyrights and patents are a decidedly imperfect tool to promote creativity, and they get increasingly imperfect the longer and more widely they are applied. The downside to longer knowledge monopolies is less follow-on creativity by everyone but the intellectual property right holder. And even the potential benefit of stimulating creativity in the first place doesn't factor into the US Copyright Extension Act and its overseas equivalents, when we are talking about continuation of existing copyrights long after the creative process is over.

A ridiculous level of intellectual property protection at home is bad for innovation in the United States and thus for the rest of the world as well. Foisting these laws on the rest of the world significantly compounds the negative economic impact. In truth, it's not so bad for development prospects if Afghan kids are forced to spend $15 on their "authentic" DVD of *Peter Pan* rather than $5 on the pirated version—that hardly sounds like the basis for a poverty trap, and it is extremely unlikely to have knock-on effects on US growth and quality of life. But lobbying by Disney and Hollywood in favor of tougher knowledge monopolies in general has a far more widespread impact than that. Not least, stricter intellectual property laws deny those who can't afford them access to the textbooks, technical manuals, and journal articles that are the basis for fostering new creativity. Reports from African universities, for example, suggest that learning materials are primarily accessed through activities that infringe on copyright. If we want more *global* innovation and creativity, we *all* need access to ideas, so there is a global cost to a high price in their transmission.[7]

And as more and more creative activity moves to countries like China, the short-term mercantilist benefit of pushing our own excessive intellectual property rights standards on the rest of the world will become an ever-greater burden on the US economy itself. After all, new material copyrighted in 2015 will only enter the public domain in 2135—by which time the West will be a bit player in the global creative process. We in the West will suffer the most from the restrictive rules we put in place—and push as global norms—today. Now is the time to be pushing for global adherence to copyrights and patents under fair and economically rational terms, before it is the West's own ability to create that is most endangered.

Intellectual property and tobacco are just two examples of a broader trend: a US trade policy that has been hijacked by special interests, including Hollywood, Detroit, and the farm and tobacco lobbies. These special interests are significantly reducing the potential benefit of open trade for the US consumer and stymieing a global trade deal that would have far greater economic impacts than poorly designed regional and bilateral approaches.

The problem (and the result) is similar in Europe. Abandoning the WTO is a failure of governance by the West as a whole.

o   o   o

STILL, THERE ARE REAL domestic issues with a global free trade agenda that require more from Western governments than the ability to negotiate a strong WTO deal. We need a policy package that allows workers to respond to the impact of greater competition and technological change in the sectors where they currently work. This should involve actually helping workers find new jobs, and it is something that the US federal government in particular has been awful at supporting.

MIT economist David Autor's work suggests that the Federal Trade Adjustment Assistance Program—the system set up to help displaced workers acquire new skills for new jobs—did little to help people adjust to greater competition from imports between 1990 and 2007. Each $1,000 in growth in Chinese imports per US manufacturing worker across US regions was associated with just twenty-three cents per adult in additional trade adjustment assistance, he suggests. Compare that to Social Security disability payments, in-kind medical benefits, and other assistance and retirement benefits, which increased by a total of $47 per $1,000 in growth in Chinese imports per exposed worker. In short, the evidence suggests that about one in four hundred federal dollars helped workers retrain out of exposed industries and the other $399 helped them retire or invalid out of those industries and the workforce completely.[8]

That didn't need to happen, as suggested by the experience of Germany over a similar period. Wolfgang Dauth and his colleagues, writing for Germany's Institute for the Study of Labor, looked at the country's rising trade with Eastern Europe and China. They concluded that import-competing industries did suffer job losses, just as in the United States. But in stark contrast to the United States, the losses were not as large as the job *gains* by German export-oriented firms. Over the period 1988 to 2008, global trade integration led to the creation of 493,000 additional German manufacturing jobs, they suggest. Furthermore, in Germany the regions that lost *manufacturing* employment to import competition didn't see rising unemployment—again, in contrast to US regions in the same position. German measures to retain, retrain, or help workers move to new job opportunities were a lot more effective than the US Trade Adjustment Assistance Program.[9]

Beyond training and transitional support, workers need new jobs to apply for—and inward investment is one important source. But that means abandoning tough-guy posturing over the risk posed by foreign firms to national security. For example, on September 28, 2012, President Obama blocked an overseas investment by the Chinese Sany Group in a series of wind farms in Oregon because the project was in close proximity to a US naval base. And a week later the Republican-led House Intelligence Committee suggested that Chinese telecom firms Huawei and ZTE were a potential threat to national security. Despite having no evidence of wrongdoing to report, the committee suggested that the administration "block acquisitions, takeovers, or mergers involving Huawei and ZTE" and that the government should not use the companies' equipment for fear it would be compromised by Chinese intelligence services.[10]

For all we may not want to use Chinese-made equipment in sensitive government communications systems, the broader distrust of ZTE and Huawei is a shame for the American consumer. The two are among the world's most innovative companies. Indeed, in 2011 they were first and third worldwide in the number of company-sponsored patent applications they made. ZTE alone made 2,826 applications, according to the World Intellectual Property Rights Organization. But it is also a shame for workers displaced by Chinese export competition—after all, Huawei employed 1,700 people in fourteen US offices and sourced parts worth $6.6 billion from American companies (compared to US sales of $1.3 billion), suggesting that the firm is a particularly odd target for politicians who are supposedly laser-focused on jobs.[11]

At the same time, since more profitable US firms can create more jobs here at home, we ought to be encouraging domestic investors to invest more overseas by providing additional support for overseas investment guarantee agencies—which help insure domestic investors against the political risks of investing abroad. The US Overseas Private Investment Corporation, for example, provides loans and political risk insurance to US firms that want to invest in the developing world and has supported cumulative investments worth over $200 billion—all while running a profit. The US Congress could expand the Corporation's operations by allowing it to back any project that is likely to have a net positive (or negligible) impact on US jobs—rather than the current rules, which ban investments that cost one US job even if they create ten more. And spreading portfolios overseas could not only increase the returns that pension funds and other institutional investors make with our money but also reduce the risks. So we should scrap limits on the proportion of public and private pension fund portfolios that can be placed abroad.

o o o

BUT EVEN THOUGH BETTER international trade and financial policies could help create jobs, lower prices, and strengthen Western economies, they aren't going to be the biggest factor in extending the West's quality of life into the future. That's because trade and finance are where we've already made considerable progress in creating a global system that fosters mutually beneficial exchange. Contrast that with migration—where progress has been minimal but its importance to continued Western economic strength is immense.

Just before the First World War, global trade reached a historically unprecedented value of around 20 percent of world GDP. Today that percentage has doubled—meaning that there has been a thirtyfold increase in the absolute volume of trade since 1913. Money moves much more easily today too. It used to take ships full of doubloons under constant threat of pirate attack or poor weather to get wealth from one place to another. But now we have electronic transfers—trillions of dollars cross borders daily.

The modern world also sees an immense amount of short-term international travel. The air transport industry moves 2.75 billion passengers a year. But a scant two million people move for the longer term from the developing to the developed world each year. That adds up to about one-thirty-fourth of annual population growth in developing regions. And migration—unlike trade and finance—has stagnated at the same level it had in the age of the horse and buggy. In the years before the First World War, legal immigration to the United States averaged over one million people a year. That's about the same absolute number as in the last few years, at a time when the US population is three times as big as it was in 1913 and the rest of the world's population is closer to four times as big.[12]

The relative extent of the globalization of things, money, ideas, and people is largely driven by Western policy decisions. For goods, average tariff rates dropped from 40 percent around World War II to less than 4 percent today among OECD countries. Along with rapidly declining logistics costs, that decrease represents significantly reduced barriers to trade. With finance, we have moved from capital controls to open currency exchanges. But when it comes to the flow of people, we've seen the West keep on throwing up more and more barriers to movement—attempts to bar not just permanent migration (think the border fence) but even weeklong visits to Sea World.

That is going to change. Because as US and European populations age, we have seen that the West will be crying out for young foreigners to fill jobs—and the competition to attract those foreigners will grow increasingly intense.

o   o   o

AT FIRST SIGHT, it might look like the United States and Europe face an embarrassment of riches when it comes to potential migrants. A Gallup survey from a couple of years ago suggested that a total of 700 million people worldwide claim they would want to relocate permanently to another country if they could; of that total, 165 million cited the United States as their favorite destination. But Gallup's more recent work suggests that the numbers are down to 630 million who would move and 145 million who would move to the United States (with 150 million naming France, Germany, the United Kingdom, or Spain).[13]

The 145 million who would still choose the United States is around half of the current American population, to be sure—but that's the number who *say* they would like to move, not the number who would actually manage it, even with completely open borders. In fact, only 19 million out of the 630 million worldwide who say they might want to move are actually making the necessary preparations, like trying to get a visa. I *say* I would like to learn Spanish well enough to go and live in Latin America for a spell. Don't ask my Argentina-born father-in-law how well I'm doing at that.

The US diversity visa program suggests how much real demand for migration is lower than stated demand. The program involved a simple online application process to enter a lottery for visas to enter the United States. In 2009 it was open to citizens of any country that didn't already have high levels of immigration to the United States, and so eligible applicants were a combined population of nearly three billion people from countries that included Brazil, China, Ecuador, India, Mexico, Pakistan, Peru, the Philippines, Poland, South Korea, and Vietnam. Just adding the simple extra step of requiring an online application considerably reduced interest. The diversity visa program had 12.1 million qualified entries—with potential dependents, the number was 16.5 million. That's an application rate of 0.55 percent of the eligible world's population—or a bit above 5 percent of the US population. Interest is surely suppressed by the fact that the success rate is measured in fractions of a percent, but it still suggests that the majority of people who say they might move to the United States really wouldn't move there because of the cost and complexity of the move, or because they'd miss family or friends, or just out of pure inertia. If the United States loosened restrictions, immigration would surely rise, but not to tsunami-like levels.[14]

In fact, the problem may soon become one of trying to attract needed talent, as recent trends in both undocumented and student migration to the United States attest. International applications to US graduate schools only just returned to their levels of 2002–2003 after a post-9/11 slump related to the economy and toughened immigration procedures, but also to growing competition from other destinations and home universities. The OECD suggests that, in absolute numbers, the United States still led the world in attracting foreign students in 2009, with 18 percent of the global total. But that had dropped from 23 percent in 2000 and left US colleges and universities as a whole with less than two-thirds of the OECD average foreign student enrollment.[15]

After they earn their diploma, Vivek Wadhwa reports in *The Immigrant Exodus,* an unprecedented number of Indian and Chinese students in the United States for further education intend to go home rather than try to stay in the United States to work. Partially as a result of growing rates of return among recent graduates, the proportion of high-tech start-ups founded by Chinese and Indian immigrants in Silicon Valley dropped from 52 percent in 2005 to 44 percent in 2011. China and India are growing rapidly, and opportunities in both countries are expanding. Meanwhile, getting a good visa to the United States is getting harder. More and more foreign graduates are asking, "Why bother?"[16]

And it isn't just potential immigrants at the high-skilled end asking this question. Arrests of undocumented immigrants along the Mexican border are at their lowest level since the 1970s—at a little over 300,000 people in 2010, or about one-fifth of their peak in 2000. In fact, the size of the undocumented immigrant population has been declining since 2007, by about 200,000 a year, according to the Pew Hispanic Center. Supply is way down primarily because the jobs that undocumented workers used to take—in construction not least—are scarce nowadays, while opportunities back at home are getting better; tougher enforcement has also played a part. As a result, we've seen states like Georgia have lost millions of dollars in crops rotting in the fields for lack of pickers.[17]

Again, this isn't just an American problem. Just like the United States, the United Kingdom is suffering reverse-migration to India, with about 300,000 Indians employed overseas expected to return home by 2015. Over time the competition for new immigrants is going to become intense. Some countries, including the United Kingdom, Australia, and Canada, have already taken steps to ease the visa process for foreign students and innovators. Spain is one of many countries offering residency in return for buying a house. This is the start of a trend, and it would be wise for Western countries further behind in attracting immigrants to catch up while they can.

o   o   o

SO WHY NOT OPEN BORDERS wider today? Much of the opposition is due to misinformed voters who misdirect their anger about inequality and lack of opportunity at immigrants. But even supposedly well-meaning and well-informed people in the West call for immigration restrictions on educated workers from the developing world on the grounds that if they can leave their home countries, they'll abandon those countries to poverty and deprivation.

As a result, the United Kingdom's National Health Service (NHS), for example, has a code of practice that bans recruitment from 150 developing countries, and there have been calls for something similar in the United States. But those selfless global thinkers promoting the curtailment of the human right to leave one's country of birth are wrong—and their rhetoric damages development prospects in rich and poor countries alike.[18]

First off, migrants make more money abroad than they would at home. John Gibson at the University of Waikato and David McKenzie of the World Bank document salary increases ranging from $40,000 to $60,000 a year for skilled emigrants from developing countries. And the migrants send a lot of that money home. The average African-trained member of the American Medical Association (AMA) sends home $6,000 a year in remittances year in and year out, for two decades or longer. That has a real impact on home economies. One estimate from the United Nations Conference on Trade and Development (UNCTAD) suggests that doubling remittances to a developing country could reduce poverty in that country by nearly one-third.[19]

Second, migrants encourage people in sending countries to get educated. Michael Clemens at the Center for Global Development finds no evidence that the "medical brain drain" from developing countries as doctors and nurses move to rich countries leads to shortages of medical staff in those developing countries, probably because the opportunity to migrate is one of the things that attracts people to medical school in the first place. For years, nurses have left the Philippines in huge numbers to work abroad, but the country still has more nurses per person than the United Kingdom.[20]

And of course many migrants eventually return home. That forty-six sitting heads of government from around the world in 2010 had been educated in the United States suggests the value of the United States educating foreigners, both to the United States itself and to those who travel to study here.[21] Again, Bill Easterly of New York University and Ariell Reshef of the University of Virginia carried out an informal survey of the entrepreneurs behind African global export successes and suggested that one factor many had in common was experience living abroad—usually in the country to which they subsequently exported.[22]

○   ○   ○

SO IT IS TIME TO ABANDON the misinformed selfish reasons against migration and the even more misinformed altruistic reasons against letting people in. What does this mean for the United States? Go back to the days when it was widely understood that America was a country built on immigration and that it would never have been the world's largest economy without it. Abandon our patchwork system based on various quotas and follow Nobel Prize–winning economist Gary Becker's advice: set an entry tariff. Rather than saying, "We'll give 85,000 places to skilled immigrants," say, "We'll let anyone in who can pay $50,000 to Uncle Sam and pass a criminal background check."

That will allow the immigrant supply to respond to demand—if farmers in Georgia or software firms in Silicon Valley find there's a significant enough shortage of potential employees in the United States, they can just loan $50,000 to more immigrants to come in. And while the money currently spent on the quota system—not least for legal fees, which can run into the tens of thousands of dollars for applicants—goes to run bureaucracy and pad lawyers' bank accounts, tariff revenues could be used to support low-income native workers through initiatives like the Earned Income Tax Credit (EITC). That would reduce the political opposition to migration among those who see themselves as most at risk from it. A $50,000 tariff applied to one million migrants (about one-third of 1 percent of the US population) would be enough to almost double the size of the EITC program.

Those who oppose the very idea of selling citizenship or residence might want to look at existing laws: the current EB-5 visa program gives green cards to people who invest $500,000 and create at least ten jobs. And the proposed (bipartisan) Schumer-Lee bill would provide a residency visa for anyone who simply spends $500,000 toward the purchase of a house, following the Spanish model. So Republicans and Democrats alike in Congress have already established what kind of immigration system the United States runs—all that's left to haggle over is the price.

To help ensure that the tariff system gives poorer migrants a shot at entry, and given the benefits of legal working status in the United States, businesses that want to see more immigrants enter could set up lending or subsidy services. Or perhaps a new development arm of the US government could finance loans for migrants from low-income countries. Regardless, tariffs should not be the only way to hand out permanent residence or citizenship. Spouses and immediate family of existing citizens, for example, should surely still get green card rights—and both students and temporary workers should be exempted.

But for a country that champions the cause of free enterprise worldwide, America's immigration system looks like it was designed by a failing-grade student of Soviet planning. Letting the market work and setting a fair price on the chance to make it big in America would reap immense benefits to both the US and the global economy. And over time, to further increase the benefit of immigration to the US economy, the tariff rate should drop.

Meanwhile, Europe has two options to expand immigrant access. First, it could expand the European Union, and second, the EU countries could increase the number of visas they give to non-EU residents. Both are highly attractive ideas that will make considerably more difference at this point to the long-term quality of life in the region than fostering an ever-deeper union among existing members.

Not letting more migrants into the West is delaying the economic recovery and costing Americans and Europeans jobs. It is damaging our long-term prospects in innovation and entrepreneurship, putting at greater risk the sustainability of programs like Social Security and Medicare, the National Health Service, and pensions, and concentrating the burden of Western debt on a declining number of working-age people. If this were better understood—and spelled out—by political leaders in the West, the challenges of migration reform might well decline.

o o o

WHAT ABOUT MOVEMENT the other way—out of the West? When it comes to exporting Americans in particular, one barrier is that language abilities in the United States are dire. Only about 14 percent of Americans claim they can speak Spanish well enough to hold a conversation. A little over 4 percent can chat in French, and less than 3 percent can converse in German. Fewer than one in a hundred Americans can converse in any other language.[23]

Yet the percentage of US elementary and middle schools offering foreign language instruction fell between 1997 and 2008—from 75 percent to 58 percent in the case of middle schools, according to the Center for Applied Linguistics. On top of that, the number of languages offered also declined. For example, French was offered at nearly half of US middle schools in 1997, but eleven years later fewer than one-quarter were offering French instruction. Chinese did better than that, but only just: a little more than 2 percent of middle schools now offer the language, up from below 1 percent in 1997. The US Department of Education has an obvious role to play in filling a gap that relates to national economic potential. Why not subsidize state provision of high school language classes?[24]

And at the college level, we've seen that US undergraduates overseas account for only 0.4 percent of the global total of people going abroad for their tertiary education—and nearly half of those brave enough to venture outside America's borders only go as far as the United Kingdom. That hardly counts as exotic in an era when Brits win half the Oscars and present the Golden Globes every year. As well as being a potential national security issue, a denuded flow of students in and out of the United States reduces the country's ability to trade, invest, and exchange technology internationally.

All of which suggests that the government ought to be helping the more intrepid American high school graduates to enroll in college abroad. Why not change the requirements for institutional participation in federal student aid programs to allow foreign schools to provide support to US student tuition and living costs? Or expand study abroad programs like the Gilman Scholarship to cover full-degree programs overseas? Or perhaps most effective: why not advertise the fact that, in most of the rest of the world, the legal drinking age is eighteen?

At the advanced-degree level, the Fulbright Program awarded approximately six thousand grants in 2008 to US students, teachers, professionals, and scholars to study, teach, lecture, and conduct research in more than 155 countries, and to their foreign counterparts to engage in similar activities in the United States. Yemen, for example, has seen 70 visiting US scholars since the Fulbright's inception, and 426 Yemenis have come to the United States under the program. The cost to the US government is about

$32,000 per awardee per year. It is an incredibly cheap and effective way to build links with the rest of the world and could be considerably expanded, as could similar programs in Europe.[25]

It is also time to ramp up the Peace Corps and similar volunteer agencies in Europe. The Peace Corps program has been invaluable in creating a stock of tens of thousands of Americans who really understand life in the developing world, just as Voluntary Services Overseas has been useful in the United Kingdom. But the current bureaucratic model of the Peace Corps—a standardized two-year volunteering package—limits the number of countries where the agency can operate and reduces demand for both volunteers and slots: the application-to-acceptance ratio is only three to one.

And because of its semi-official nature, the program is expensive. Private-sector volunteer programs can provide placement for $5,000 to $6,000 a year, which is about 10 percent of the cost per Peace Corps volunteer. Given all of that, it would make considerable sense for the Peace Corps to move toward awarding grants for overseas service, on the model of the Fulbrights, rather than attempting to provide a full volunteer package. That would allow the program to considerably expand, without increasing its budget, and attract a wider array of volunteers to go to more countries.

o   o   o

WHAT ABOUT LATER IN LIFE? We've seen that a growing number of Germans are retiring across Europe thanks in part to the fact that they can easily take their benefits with them. Why not try the same thing in the United States? If the country made benefits more easily portable to Mexico or Thailand, for instance, it would save money on health care and improve retirees' quality of life.

Health care in particular could see huge cost savings through greater mobility. Total health care expenditures in the United States in 2009 topped $2.5 trillion, or nearly 18 percent of GDP. And the efficiency of all that spending appears pretty low. According to World Bank data, Costa Rica and the United States have the same life expectancy (seventy-nine years), but Costa Rica spends only 16 percent of the US amount per head on health services. So if some American Medicare recipients moved to Costa Rica, perhaps they could enjoy the same level of health at a lower cost to the US taxpayer. There is certainly the demand: a survey of retired Americans living in Mexico found that 96 percent said that they would seek medical services in the country if Medicare covered it.

Medicare and Medicaid could also cover services abroad for people who travel to get those services and pay the travel costs. The US military and veterans' health care plans already cover treatment abroad, but civilians are not so lucky. Similarly, European health services could promise to reimburse nationals for necessary procedures carried out at less cost abroad.

Medical tourism will remain a niche product. Some of the most expensive medical care is long-term and end-of-life. It would be difficult to outsource that health care to other countries because most people who are in the hospital for a long time want to be close to family and friends. And for some complex treatments, the best doctors—or the only qualified doctors—may be in the United States or Europe. That means that the considerable majority of Medicare/Medicaid and National Health Service costs would remain at home even if the programs covered travel and overseas treatment.

Still, the savings from government-sponsored foreign care could be big. A 2008 report by the Deloitte Center for Health

Solutions forecast the growth of medical tourism from the United States. Its low-end estimates were that $26 billion would be spent on US health tourism by 2015 for procedures that would have cost $195 billion to perform in the United States. This suggests $169 billion in savings. If Medicaid and Medicare changed their rules and only saved the same proportion of that low-end estimate as their share of total US health expenditures, and that change had absolutely no impact on creating additional demand for medical tourism, that would add up to $60 billion in savings in 2015.[26]

o o o

MORE OPEN WESTERN TRADING REGIMES with lower protections for monopolies and public bads like smoking, combined with free investment flows and the freer movement of people, will, of course, be in the huge interests of the Rest. But we have seen that what is good for the Rest is good for the West as well because, like it or not, the West needs the rest of the world—and global cooperation—more than ever if it is to preserve its greatness. While the West still has its dominance, it should use that dominance to shape global institutions to be more favorable to ex-hegemons and other economies not at the top of the global GDP rankings. It is time for US politicians in particular to recognize how much more the country can achieve in partnership than in isolation. That partnership is discussed in the next chapter.

CHAPTER NINE

Sustaining Global Progress

MOST NORMAL AMERICANS APPEAR quite willing to take part in nonmilitary multilateral efforts to make the world a more peaceful place rather than carry the burden alone. Forty percent of Americans think the country relies too much on its military strength to achieve foreign policy goals, compared to 10 percent who believe it relies too little on military strength. And as an example of willingness to sign on to international agreements, 70 percent think America should be part of the International Criminal Court.[1]

These opinions only reflect attitudes that have long dominated in the United States. Generous global partnership for selfish reasons used to be the standard approach of policymakers as well. That economic advance in other parts of the world is good for the United States was the insight behind the Marshall Plan, behind the original US-backed creation of the International Monetary Fund and the World Bank, and behind the US lead taken on trade negotiations that reduced tariffs and quotas. Between 1945 and 1975, average US import tariffs on dutiable goods fell from nearly 30 percent to around 8 percent, for example, despite the fact that the US role in the global economy was so dominant that, according to traditional trade theory, there could have been domestic benefits to a tariff regime. All of this generous multilateralism stemmed from a realization that a robust global economy underpinned by strong institutions of global cooperation was in the long-term interest of the United States.

Later on, the United States supported the development of the European Coal and Steel Community—which eventually evolved into the European Union—on the same grounds. Some saw the EU as a competitor to the United States, but the benefits of a strong, stable Europe to the US economy and national security outweighed such concerns. The change from the multilateralism of the recent past to today's paranoid fear of treaty enforcement by UN black helicopters is a pretty sad condition for what is supposedly still the world's only superpower.

It is particularly sad because multilateralism makes even more sense in the future. To constrain the behavior of rising economic superpowers, the United States should be embracing international institutions and strengthening global cooperation and norms to help bind China, India, and Brazil more firmly into an open economic system that will become ever more vital to Western prospects. The United States and the European Union both should use their limited remaining time at the top of global economic rankings to make sure that global economic institutions are both secure and fair to those *not* in the top spots—because soon enough those are the spots that will be occupied by the countries of the West.

Two recent examples show how far Washington is from understanding the benefits of multilateralism today. In 2012 the US Senate voted down ratification of the United Nations Convention on the Rights of Persons with Disabilities. The Convention, already ratified by 126 countries worldwide, is designed to help protect the 700 million–odd people on the planet with a disability from discrimination and to improve their access to education, services, and employment. It is based on the language and ideals of the pathbreaking Americans with Disabilities Act of 1990. That may be why the US Chamber of Commerce likes the treaty. The Chamber was opposed to the Americans with Disabilities Act back in 1990, but it lives in hope that the global treaty will foist the costs of compliance that the Chamber never wanted for American businesses on firms from other countries. Despite all of that, fear of the United Nations in the Senate doomed passage.

Then there's the United Nations Convention on the Law of the Sea, which came into force in 1994. It creates rules for maritime activities, from rights to mining on the ocean floor to shipping lanes in international waters. The Law of the Sea has been ratified by 161 countries—but not the United States, despite the fact that the Chamber of Commerce (again), the National Association of Manufacturers, Republican and Democratic secretaries of state alike from Kissinger onward, and pretty much everyone with a star in the Pentagon wants the United States to sign up. One result of ratifying the treaty would be securing 4.1 million miles of ocean floor for US jurisdiction. It would be a useful tool in the effort to peacefully resolve disputes over the South China Sea. And signing would give US firms more secure rights to mine and drill in parts of the Arctic. But the fortress mentality in the Senate has proven too strong once again.

These two examples are only the tip of the iceberg. International agreements covering women's rights and land mines are among the other treaties written in ways that the United States supports but abandoned because they are presented in a UN binder. The iceberg refuses to melt: also frozen are agreements on global trade, the global financial system, and the environment. The intransigence of US lawmakers has also immobilized what may be the greatest moral responsibility of the West and the nouveau riche nations in the Rest: to ensure that *everyone* around the world benefits (sustainably) from the awesome wealth of the planet by eliminating the scourge of absolute poverty.

But that attitude has to change—multilateral solutions provide the surest path to sustainable global growth and stability. Countries of the Rest have been opening up to trade, providing resources to international financial institutions, providing aid, and investing in renewables. The United States and Europe should use multilateral institutions to lock in that good citizenship while they still have time. The West should swap its control of many of these multilateral bodies for the Rest's commitment to support multilateral approaches into the future.

○   ○   ○

TAKE TRADE: THE WEST IS STANDING in the way of a global trade deal largely at the insistence of special interests, not least of which are an agriculture lobby addicted to billions in subsidies and "creative industries" addicted to knowledge monopolies. But there's an increasingly urgent need to update WTO rules to reflect the new realities of global trade: production chains and a growing trade in services. This is an agenda that can't be handled under regional deals, if only because production chains span regions.

The growing trade in services in particular links back to the movement of people: a company providing consulting services across borders is usually moving staff to provide them. Of course, just as the United States and Europe restrict such movement, so do the nations of the Rest. This suggests that it may be time to start multilateral negotiations on temporary migration, with an eye to matching agreements on trade and investment already under the WTO umbrella. It is in the self-interest of the United States and Europe to begin these negotiations now, when there is little doubt that the greater pressure for movement overall is from the Rest to the West. Much like the United States launching international trade negotiations under the General Agreement on Tariffs and Trade (GATT) back at a time when by far the biggest prize was access to US markets, the West will be in a stronger bargaining position if it opens negotiations now on temporary migration.

Meanwhile, the West's stubborn commitment to former prerogatives is hampering efforts to ensure stability in the global financial system. To keep more control without spending cash, Western governments have been weakening global financial institutions, including the International Monetary Fund. The West needs a strong IMF to help pull itself out of its current fiscal and financial sector mess, including $103 billion in loans to Greece, Ireland, and Portugal to help stave off national bankruptcy and a collapsing euro. But it also needs the IMF to ensure that globalization continues on an equitable basis as the Rest becomes dominant. For example, if the US government was looking for a more powerful tool of international governance to use in the battle against an undervalued renminbi, an IMF with enhanced powers would be critical.

Despite the advantages of a strong IMF, the United States and Europe are now standing in the way of global efforts that would strengthen the legitimacy and power of this institution they were so central to creating by rebalancing voting shares on the IMF board to better reflect global economic realities. Emerging countries and oil producers have the cash to commit and want to increase their voting shares on the board that oversees the IMF (just like a listed company, the IMF determines votes by shares), while Europe and the United States don't want to give up that power and won't commit additional funds to keep the balance of shares in their favor. Like an idiot venture capitalist interested in control more than in company success, Western shareholders would rather keep the IMF small but theirs than let it get big, but with ownership diffused through the sale of additional shares— even if that means the Fund is worth much less to everyone on the planet, including the West, as a result.

Even after recent hard-fought adjustments, voting shares will look decidedly antiquated. The BRICS (Brazil, Russia, India, China, and South Africa) as a whole will have 14 percent of IMF voting power, compared to 29 percent for the EU, despite the fact that using a measure that averages market and purchasing power measures of GDP, the two groups are the same size. Using GDP measures that fully account for the fact that you can buy more for your money in developing countries, the BRICS are considerably larger. The IMF reports that the United States accounted for 20.4 percent of GDP in 2009 and 17.4 percent of the voting share under the proposed formula. China accounted for 12.6 percent of the world's GDP but has a voting share of 6.4 percent under the proposed reform.

A lame ostrich strategy of being too weak to commit additional resources but too fearful to give up votes can only last so long. Any significant revision of the IMF vote system that accounts for both economic weight and a concern about "voice" (votes for the world's poorest countries) would involve the United States losing its veto power over board decisions at the Fund— either immediately or very soon. And the West might have to abandon the clubby deal by which a European always gets selected as IMF managing director. But, a weak IMF is an immediate and vital threat to Europe. This time the IMF may be able to borrow enough money, even under the old share system, to prevent a euro collapse, for example. But what about the next crisis? If Europe had to give up its lock on appointing the top spot as part of a deal to make the IMF a stronger institution, that would be a small price to pay.

It isn't just the IMF where the West is trying to preserve party host influence in a global institution while contributing less than a potluck share of resources. In 2010, when it came to the latest giving round to the World Bank's soft-loan arm, the International Development Association, the United States gave 12.1 percent of total funds. That compares to the United Kingdom at 12 percent and Japan at 10.9 percent. Canada, with an economy about one-ninth the size of the US economy (smaller than California's), gave 4.1 percent—a threefold-larger contribution per dollar of GDP. Yet the United States retains a veto on the World Bank's board as well—and its own lock on appointing the institution's president. The West should agree with emerging economies like India and China: we will give you more votes if you provide more cash to the International Development Association.

o o o

THE REST HAS AN INDISPENSABLE role to play in preserving the global environment as well. China is now the largest greenhouse gas emitter in the world—emitting more carbon per capita than does Sweden. Again, Russia's emissions of carbon dioxide per citizen are considerably higher than France's, Germany's, or the United Kingdom's. But the rich world owes the greatest obligation to deal with the climate issue because the West still accounts for the majority of carbon dioxide pumped into the atmosphere by humanity.[2] We've seen that a lot of progress has been made by individual US states, the European Union, and developing countries around the world acting at best in partial coordination. But a multilateral treaty that recognized both the responsibilities of rich countries and the vital participation of developing countries in reducing greenhouse gas emissions would be better.

There is a lot of work to be done by the new rich and old rich alike to move toward policies that will help preserve the global environment. The leaders of the G-20 nations—the twenty largest economies—have made a start by agreeing to cut fossil fuel subsidies. The International Energy Agency suggests that removing these subsidies worldwide would reduce carbon dioxide emissions by as much as 2.6 gigatons a year by 2035, or about half the emissions reductions required to keep the planet on a warming trajectory that peaks below two degrees Centigrade in average temperature increases.[3]

Indirect subsidies to fossil fuels, including tax breaks and favorable access to land, are still worth $45 billion to $70 billion in the OECD club of rich nations alone. For example, uncompetitive US federal auctions of coal-mining rights in Montana and Wyoming's Powder River Basin alone may have cost taxpayers up to $30 billion over the past thirty years (or sixty times the cost of loan guarantees to Solyndra, the solar panel manufacturer whose failure caused such a stink in 2012).

Meanwhile, climate-damaging, food-price-increasing American biofuel production is sustained only through regulatory fiat that requires minimum ethanol levels in fuel. The United States diverted more than 80 million tons of corn into ethanol production in 2008.[4] Looking forward, the United Nations Food and Agriculture Organization has estimated that grain prices in 2018 will be 14 percent higher than they would be otherwise if their prediction that biofuel production will double by then proves correct.[5]

Again, moves like the US Commerce Department's anti-dumping complaints and 30 percent tariffs on Chinese solar panel imports are shortsighted at best. The United States is blessed with considerably better sites for locating solar panels in terms of cloud cover and latitude than many OECD countries, including Germany, but it still lags far behind them in solar energy production. Rather than spending time making solar panel imports more expensive, why not save money, the climate, and national security concerns by taking on Big Fossil?

The United States should lock in reform by committing to considerable reductions in greenhouse gases as part of a global treaty. And the West as a whole should live up to its commitments to pay some of the costs of renewable energy rollout in the developing world. After all, the OECD is asking poorer economies to take a different and more expensive path to development than it did in order to save Venice, coral reefs, and the polar bear for everyone. In return, the West could ask the Rest to lock into lower-carbon growth trajectories as the only way to forestall runaway climate change going forward. Such a deal would cost the West money. But the amounts involved are likely still to be lower than the resources created by one solid year's worth of global economic growth. That seems a small price to pay for global environmental sustainability.

o o o

ANOTHER CONSEQUENCE OF a rising Rest is that fewer countries are going to need large quantities of development assistance. The number of countries classified by the World Bank as low-income—an average income less than about $1,000 per year—fell from sixty-three to thirty-five from 2000 to 2010. And between now and 2025, the number of countries with an average income below $1,165 (the current cutoff to receive very-low-interest IDA loans from the World Bank) may fall from sixty-eight countries (with a population of three billion) to thirty-one countries) with a population of one billion), according to Todd Moss and Ben Leo at the Center for Global Development.[6] In the longer term, that could free up resources to support moves toward clean energy in the developing world.

But given the West's large and growing interest in ensuring that the Rest becomes healthy, educated, and set on a sustainable path to prosperity, rich countries should still do all that they can to encourage sustained development in the countries that are home to the planet's most disadvantaged. For example, millions of kids worldwide still die from easily preventable diseases each year. That's not just an ethical disaster—involving as it does so many avoidable child deaths—but a drag on global improvements in the quality of life as ill health spills over across countries (not least through infectious disease transmission) and slows broader progress in the developing world.

The most powerful tools to transform poor countries and poor people into rich ones are those discussed in previous chapters: open trade, finance, migration, and the free flow of ideas. While there is a vital role for aid, we should also recognize its limits. In 2010, according to the OECD, the United States gave $30 billion in aid, or about 0.2 percent of US GDP.

In that year the GDP of low- and middle-income countries was a little over $20 *trillion* at market prices, according to the World Bank, making US aid equivalent to about 0.15 percent of developing-country GDP. Expenditure worth an average of somewhat less than one-six-hundredth of recipient countries' economies is unlikely to buy peace, democracy, open markets, and more rapid growth.[7]

That's not to say aid doesn't work. Used right, aid can achieve remarkable things. Aid flows have helped save tens of millions of lives, been instrumental in getting tens of millions of kids into school, and helped build water and sewage lines, roads, and electricity networks serving millions more. Take the incredibly rapid decline we're seeing in child deaths in Africa over the past decade. In Kenya, for example, the proportion of kids dying before the age of five fell from 12 percent in 2003 to 7 percent in 2008; thanks to the declining mortality rate just over that period, 63,000 more Kenyan kids born this year will live to their fifth birthday. World Bank research suggests that the spread of insecticide-treated bed-nets to fight malaria played a huge role in that decline. The number of nets in use in sub-Saharan Africa climbed from 5.6 million in 2004 to 145 million in 2010, according to UNICEF. Most of those bed-nets were provided by aid programs.[8]

But most aid is not that effective, in part because all too much aid follows a model of giving developing countries and poor people stuff we don't want—like surplus grain, used T-shirts, and unsolicited advice and opinions. A new model would be one of partnering with countries and the world's poorest to give them what they need most—money—in a way that targets specific public goods (from vaccine coverage to learning in school) and specific people (the very poorest).

The blog Tales from the Hood, run by an anonymous aid worker, responded to the proclivity of charities and aid agencies to hand over goods and services we wouldn't use to recipients in developing countries who never asked for what they get by setting up the SWEDOW (Stuff WE DOn't Want) prize for aid. The initial SWEDOW prize was won by Knickers for Africa, an organization that sent "gently used" panties south of the Sahara. But SWEDOW is the gift of choice in the aid industry more broadly. Perhaps the mother of all SWEDOWs is the $2 billion–plus US food aid program—a thoroughly discredited form of assistance that lingers on only because of the lobbying muscle of agriculture conglomerates.

US aid researchers John Norris and Connie Viellette report that US food shipped abroad in response to humanitarian disasters usually arrives four to six months after the crisis begins; the US Government Accountability Office (GAO) suggests that buying the food locally would be 25 percent cheaper and the food could be delivered in about one-quarter of the time it takes to arrive from the United States.[9] Getting food to a famine area a little bit faster than six months after people start to starve really might be a good idea. Regardless, Amartya Sen's work has conclusively shown that people rarely die of starvation or malnutrition because of an absolute lack of food in the neighborhood or the country; rather, they die because they can't afford to buy the food that's available. Sending money rather than food just works better.[10]

Even a lot of development assistance provided in the form of cash is predicated on reform ("you'll only get the money if you cut the civil service wage bill," for instance). But unwanted policy advice from expensive consultants and policy conditions on aid flows are also forms of SWEDOW. Unasked-for advice to ministers and civil society on what to do works about as well as unwanted advice to anyone on sartorial choices or careers—this according to an analysis of "policy-based lending" by New York University's Bill Easterly. Even if supposedly tied to aid flows, such advice is just routinely ignored.[11]

On the other hand, we know from repeated experiments that if you just hand money to very poor people, they'll use it to improve their diet, put their kids in school, or pay for health care. It is an incredibly powerful tool for development. So with food aid or consultants, much as with shirts, shoes, or even gently used panties, the first question to ask is: why wouldn't it be better just to give people money? And thanks to a declining number of the absolute poor worldwide, combined with better technologies to target poor people directly, it is increasingly plausible just to hand money directly to everyone worldwide living at or near $1.25 a day.[12]

Brookings scholars Laurence Chandy and Geoffrey Gertz suggest that if we could have accurately and directly supplemented the income of each poor person in the world in 2005 to bring their daily income up to $1.25, it would have cost $96 billion. By 2010, as the number of poor people fell, that cost had dropped to $66 billion. Double that number to allow for inaccurate targeting and program costs and it about equals the current value of global aid flows. As developing countries continue to grow, the cost of buying the poor out of absolute poverty would continue to drop.[13]

Of course, there is a lot more to poverty than lack of money. The immense strides that the world has made in vaccinating kids and protecting them from malaria using bed-nets are a sign of the huge role played by aid in the non-income dimensions of poverty. But even here there might be a reason to move from providing stuff to providing money. Rather than providing vaccination project designs and vaccines, for instance, it might be better sometimes to say to governments, "We'll pay you $100 million if we get independent verification that you've increased the coverage rate for a basic package of child vaccines from 50 percent of children under five to 60 percent of children. And we'll pay you $200 million if you reach 70 percent coverage." This model is called "cash on delivery" aid—because the money is transferred only if the recipient country delivers results. Donors can be sure their money has an impact because they pay out only if the result is achieved. And recipient governments are free to experiment to find the most effective way to deliver those results.

Without increasing aid budgets at all, moving from the SWEDOW model to one based on handing over cash directly to the very poorest or in return for measured improvements in the quality of life fostered by improved government service provision would considerably increase the return to donor funding. Add in support for the development of new technological innovations and experimentation in areas like off-grid renewable electricity or new vaccines and we have an aid model that could end the moral stain of absolute poverty while considerably improving the global quality of life—to the benefit of us all. If the United States and Europe committed to support such an aid regime under the World Bank and other multilateral aid agencies, and as part of the reform of voting shares, new donors, including China, would have an incentive to come on board as well.

o o o

GIVEN GROWING GLOBAL COMITY, it is not surprising that recent US national security assessments increasingly emphasize nonmilitary planetary threats like disease and climate change. Yet, in 2011, the United States spent about $768 billion on defense compared to $55 billion on the State Department, USAID, and various other foreign policy programs. Perhaps it is time to reevaluate our spending priorities. Redirecting some of the defense expenditure to high-impact development and sustainability programs — especially around efforts to prevent the spread of infectious diseases as well as efforts to shift developing economies onto a low-carbon trajectory — would dramatically reduce national security threats while strengthening the global economy for the benefit of all.

The West remains the richest region and the United States its biggest economy. It is still responsible for most of the greenhouse gases already in the atmosphere and contains the great majority of the world's wealthy population — the ones consuming resources at an unsustainable rate. Western countries still have a responsibility to lead even while the Rest should do more as well. But it is not an onerous leadership responsibility, both because it is not that expensive and because responding to the challenge of global sustainable development will create a world in which the riches and quality of life in the West will be higher than ever — and considerably higher than in an alternative world where the West fails in that leadership.

CHAPTER TEN

Life Near the Top

D URING THE 2012 Republican National Convention, New Jersey governor Chris Christie called for a "Second American Century." There is absolutely no reason why the twenty-first century should not be an "American Century" — if by that is meant America retaining or even enhancing its global reputation as a country to be emulated. America will not be the largest economy, but it really could — and should — end the twenty-first century as one of the very best places to live, ever. Europe has a similar opportunity. Indeed, compared to the previous century of war and division in the region, the twenty-first should be one of peace, expanding unity, and unprecedented quality of life.

To accomplish that requires focusing on what matters to making a country a dynamic economy. The West's leaders could learn something about that from research on why some Western cities have grown and others have declined over the past decades. University of Chicago economist Jesse Shapiro looked at US metropolitan areas to study which ones grew faster. He found that a 10 percent increase in an area's concentration of college-educated residents led to 0.8 percent faster employment growth. He suggested that a little over half of that growth was due to more rapidly rising productivity thanks to all of the smart graduates around. But 40 percent of the employment growth was due to demands from all of those graduates for improvements in the city's quality of life. In short, Shapiro found that cities with more bars and restaurants grew faster.[1]

Harvard's Ed Glaeser and his colleagues similarly found that US cities with more live performance venues and restaurants saw faster population growth in the last quarter of the twentieth century (although bowling alleys were a growth killer). They also found that urban amenities became more important to growth over time, in both the United States and Europe. The lesson: quality of life really matters to economic prospects, because nicer places attract more productive workers.[2]

And that suggests potentially great news for the West. Because compared to almost any other place or any other time, America today is just a wonderfully incredible place to live. There are far too much poverty and ill health and too many denied opportunities. But even middle-class people can buy a large house a reasonably short drive to work in a safe neighborhood with good public schools near incredibly beautiful state and federal parks. Your neighbors, more often than not, will be friendly nonjudgmental folk who bring you frozen dinners after your family has added a baby. For all the complaints about the quality of WiFi on the rather slow "fast" trains from Washington to New York, or the permanent cancellation vortex that is Chicago's O'Hare Airport, infrastructure in the country largely works. The United States has never seen a 100-kilometer-long traffic snarl-up lasting for ten days like the China National Highway Jam, for example. And partially as a result of better traffic management, no American city suffers the kind of smog that regularly blankets China's capital. The legal system in the United States is too large, but largely uncapricious. The streets are safe—even if they would be safer with fewer submachine guns in circulation. While the government may be reading your Facebook messages, you are secure in what you say. And it is easy to ignore the immense luck we enjoy, having been born in a place and an age when we can follow the religion we like, marry the people we love, and carry a man-bag without too much regard for the opinions of others.

All of the same applies to Europe, with comparatively minor differences, such as smaller, older houses and parks, more neighbors, a closer (if not necessarily shorter) commute, more historic public buildings, longer holidays, and truly universal health care. For all of the improvements in the quality of life of the Rest, Europe and America remain the most attractive places to live for most of those who would consider moving.

The West's remaining advantage in quality of life is a key to its continued progress. That advantage will allow America and Europe to continue importing talent, skills, and young people. It's surely one of the big reasons why America is the number-one location that potential migrants mention as a destination country in Gallup surveys (as we've seen), with a bunch of European countries not far behind. It is why the world's centamillionaires still favor cities in the West.

Again we've already seen that the West can leverage the advantage of a high quality of life into economic dynamism only if it lets people in. It's also true that the West can exploit that advantage only if it continues improving the quality of life of residents. And while domestic policies may have little to do with who is number one in absolute output, they have far more influence over who is number one in educational outcomes, health outcomes, incarceration rates, unemployment rates, inequality, and a range of other quality-of-life performance metrics. So, for the sake of our economic dynamism tomorrow, the West should be focusing on its quality of life today.

America has a lot of work to do to continue improving the quality of life of the average resident. According to the Congressional Budget Office, from 1979 to 2007 the richest 1 percent saw their after-tax incomes climb 275 percent, but over the same period the rise was just 18 percent for the poorest one-fifth. The median American's income actually fell by 7 percent from 1999 to 2010.[3]

It has been a bad decade for the average American on a range of non-output measures as well. Not least, there is evidence of declining health for many segments of the population. And in the United States in 2013, 7 percent were unemployed, another seven-tenths of 1 percent of the country who were in jail and 28 percent had no high school diploma. These phenomena are related. New York University economist Bill Easterly, among others, has argued that a higher share of total incomes for those in the middle of the distribution is associated with improved outcomes in health, education, stability, and growth.[4]

So fixing the inequality problem is a central element of improving overall quality of life in rich and poor countries alike. The evidence suggests that income inequality is intimately connected to a gross inequality of *opportunity* between those born to privilege and the less lucky majority. That in turn suggests a huge and unnecessary loss of talent and productivity from those denied opportunity—to the detriment of all the rest of us. According to an analysis by economists Samuel Bowles and Herbert Gintis at the Santa Fe Institute, of children born to the poorest 10 percent of parents in the United States, more than half remain in the bottom one-fifth of incomes as adults.[5] Miles Corak of Statistics Canada suggests that kids of low-income parents become low-income adults with far greater regularity in the United States than elsewhere. Fully one-half of a son's earnings can be predicted by the income of his father in the United States, compared to less than 20 percent in Canada or Scandinavia.[6]

The good news is that we know how to reverse these trends and increase opportunity for all because we have done it before. The passage of Roosevelt's New Deal legislation in the 1930s laid the basis for recovery and sustained, equitable growth over the next forty years. According to economists Thomas Piketty and Emmanuel Saez of the National Bureau of Economic Research, the top 10 percent's share of total national income dropped from around 45 percent in the 1930s to 32 percent in the postwar period and stayed at that level until the end of the 1970s.[7]

Since then, the top 10 percent's share of national income has climbed back up above 40 percent, while average growth rates have moved in the other direction. A paper by Piketty and Saez and their colleague Anthony Atkinson suggests that changing tax policies has helped bolster the share of the richest 1 percent in the United States from 9 to 15 percent of national income since 1985. Given that those tax changes were followed by a period of particularly sluggish growth for the United States, it is hardly clear that they've helped lift a rising tide for all in the form of stronger economic performance.[8]

So a new New Deal—including both regulatory reform of the financial sector and higher taxes on the rich that would pay for a better quality of education, improved infrastructure, and health services for everyone—might help propel the United States and the rest of the West back onto the high-growth, low-inequality track we derailed from in the late 1970s.

For those worried that the lessons of the 1930s don't apply in the world of the twenty-first century, taking a look south and east shows that similar rules still do work. Look at the history of the East Asian "miracle" economies like China, South Korea, and Thailand. Underpinning growth in those countries was land reform (which gave small farmers a larger share of property), alongside widespread access to health and education. That access helped ensure that everyone could play a role in generating the immense income gains that catapulted a number of countries in the region from mass poverty to membership in the OECD club of rich countries over the course of three decades.

Or more recently, from 1990 to 2008, Brazil was the leader in South America in reducing inequality. The top fifth of the population saw their share of total income decline from 65 percent to 59 percent, while the bottom two-fifths saw their share increase from 8 percent to 10 percent. Part of that progress was undoubtedly due to an innovative program called Bolsa Familia, introduced by President Lula da Silva after the 2000 election that brought him to power. The program has provided cash transfers to 12 million poor families, with part of the money conditional on parents getting their kids vaccinated and sending them to school. Payments add as much as 40 percent to the incomes of some households. Surveys suggest that most of the money is used to buy food, school supplies, and clothes for the children. Meanwhile, the conditions attached have had a dramatic impact on both vaccination rates and school enrollment among recipient families. According to an analysis by Isabel Ortiz and Matthew Cummins, the latest data suggest that the very bottom fifth of the population still controls only 3 percent of the country's income. But the last decade of progress is a start.[9]

Both the East Asian and Latin American experiences suggest that we should not be worried that middle-class people can't afford to put an en-suite in the master bedroom. Instead, we should be worried about poor people—and in particular poor kids—who can't compete on anything like a level playing field because they are excluded from the social, health, and learning opportunities that underpin success.

That suggests a potentially huge role for education in particular to level the playing field. Miles Corak argues that education plays a big role in different levels of intergenerational inequality across countries. Rich parents keep their kids in school. In countries where there are particularly high returns to education, staying in school ensures that those kids will go on to earn a lot more. Among the OECD club of rich countries, the highest payoffs to education are in France, the United States, and the United Kingdom—the countries where the link between a parent's income and a child's income is also the highest.[10]

The answer is not necessarily "more money for education"— after all, the United States, France, and the United Kingdom already spend a lot on schools. Instead, there could be a large return to focusing on young children and giving them the opportunity to be in an environment that stimulates early learning. Corak argues that universal day care is a significant factor in explaining both lower child poverty rates and higher rates of mobility in Scandinavia than in the United States.

o o o

WHAT MAKES AMERICA GREAT isn't that it has the largest GDP or the biggest military. That was not remotely true when the founding fathers crafted the work of genius that is the US Constitution. America is a country made great by the founding principles of broad-based democracy, education, civil rights, and openness embodied in that pioneering document. These principles are what make the country a shining city on the hill, whatever the presence of the odd tarnished building. And it will be a return to the founding values of equality of opportunity at home and creation of opportunity for those from elsewhere that will keep the country a great one into the future.

Similarly, what makes the EU bloc great isn't that it is quite large and that the euro, if it survives, may equal the renminbi and the dollar in global reserves. What makes the European Union great is the vision of a united continent, free of the wars that have plagued the peoples of Europe and dragged down much of the rest of the world with them, open to the movement of people and ideas in a way unimaginable since Charlemagne, united in a common endeavor of overcoming ancient rivalries for a better quality of life. And it is expanding that vision—through growing membership and open borders—that will make Europe stronger economically and socially through the twenty-first century.

More widespread educational opportunities, better health for all, and access to places with quality jobs (and quality restaurants) will help improve the economic competitiveness of both the United States and Europe. These critical ingredients of a high quality of life will also increase the West's advantage in attracting the global talent that will be more and more important in sustaining and enhancing that quality of life and making it available to ever more people, foreign- and native-born alike. The fortress mentality, by contrast, will lead only to a spiral toward disengagement and an aging, shrinking population living in increasing penury. In short, a policy based on expectations of a better world will be self-fulfilling—as will one based on anxiety. The choice is obvious.

Conclusion

ONE MOMENT THE REST is about to overtake us through unfair competition. The next moment it is a starving morass, helpless without our aid or invasion. We are either sorry for the developing countries of Africa, Latin America, and Asia or scared of them. But actually, more and more of the developing world is neither worthy of fear nor desirous of pity—it is a place of immense opportunity. Think of how countries like Britain and the United States view France—as sometimes annoying, but basically a useful partner, a great place to visit, and a source of nice things from cheese to wine to haute couture. This is how we should see the rest of the world.

Official Washington sometimes acknowledges this fact. The Obama administration's "Quadrennial Diplomacy and Development Review," for example, supports "countries' efforts to achieve sustained and broad-based economic growth, which creates opportunities for people to lift themselves, their families, and their societies out of poverty, away from violent extremism and instability, and toward a more prosperous future."[1] America's "National Security Strategy" suggests that, "through an aggressive and affirmative development agenda and commensurate resources, we can strengthen the regional partners we need to help us stop conflict and counter global criminal networks; build a stable, inclusive global economy with new sources of prosperity; advance democracy and human rights; and ultimately position ourselves to better address key global challenges by growing the ranks of prosperous, capable and democratic states that can be our partners in the decades ahead."[2]

But at the same time, when countries do actually get more prosperous, we accuse them of stealing our jobs, or our markets, or our security. Presidential candidates use foreign countries and migrants as convenient evils that can be denigrated without fear of lost votes or donations (so much more straightforward than attacking guns or tobacco). Congress fulminates against the growing influence of international treaty organizations as if they were the Trilateral Commission, the Illuminati, Opus Dei, and the Communist International all rolled into one.

At times the sophisticated foreign policy thinkers of Georgetown or Tufts are no better. International relations theory is too often presented in purely relative terms. The realist position effectively proposes that every country is solely out to be top of the pile. That's impossible for the vast majority, of course, and dumb even for the few for whom it is plausible. This isn't a zero-sum competition, and foreign policy thinking that treats the world that way is immensely counterproductive.

Congressional bluster may only be posturing, and international relations departments are full of people who actually quite like traveling overseas—and even welcome professors from other countries to come and take jobs. But counterproductive theorizing and posturing have real-world consequences when it comes to America's ability to engage globally and create the institutions it will need when there is no question it has lost its top-nation status. People in the United States want jobs and security and education and health and a clean environment. All of those things are easier to provide in a world of global partnership than they are in a world of zero-sum competition. And it is about time that message was trumpeted from the well of the House of Representatives to the halls of Columbia University.

This message is important because there is nothing inevitable in either the continued rise of the Rest or the benefits that will accrue to the West. Perhaps China's economy will crash under the weight of banking stupidity that eclipses even that of Goldman Sachs and Lehman Brothers in 2008. Perhaps rogue elements will get hold of Pakistan's tactical nuclear weapons and foment a regional nuclear war. Perhaps climate change will happen faster, with more disastrous impacts, than consensus scenarios suggest. Or perhaps the growing spread of antibiotic resistance will create a superbug that kills millions. There are many potential threats to global progress and a high quality of life that we should prepare against in partnership and with urgency and resolve. But one thing that is simply *not* a threat is continued economic and social progress in the developing world. That is an immense opportunity—and one that the West should be doing all that it can to nurture and sustain.

The opportunities of a wealthier world will also be far easier to grasp if the West stops trying to reverse the inevitable flow of its relative decline and moves to channel it instead. Rather than focusing on retaining or regaining top-nation status on anachronistic measures of influence like aggregate output, policymakers would be better employed seeking to maximize America's and Europe's benefits from a richer, healthier, more educated, and safer world.

Numerous self-help books suggest that we'd be happier and more balanced people if we spent less time worrying about status and more time enjoying what we have. That's true at the level of nation-states too. In fact, being number two or number three on a measure that doesn't matter could help America and Europe climb to number one on a bunch more measures that do. So thank your lucky stars if you were born in the West in time to witness the rise of the Rest. Because it's pretty much all upside.

Acknowledgments

Thanks to *BusinessWeek* ("Small World") and *Foreign Policy* ("The Optimist") for originally publishing some of the material presented here in columns. And thanks to Susan Glasser, Blake Hounshell, Ben Pauker, Charles Homans, Josh Keating, Margy Slattery at *FP*, and Romesh Ratnesar at *BusinessWeek* for editorial and fact-checking advice and suggestions that considerably strengthened drafts of those columns.

Thanks to colleagues at the Center for Global Development for ideas, advice, and research that inform much of what is written here—not least Amanda Glassman, Todd Moss, Michael Clemens, Kim Elliot, Bill Savedoff, Justin Sandefur, Andy Sumner, Alan Gelb, Vij Ramachandran, Sarah Dykstra, David Roodman, Jonathan Karver, Nancy Birdsall, and Arvind Subramanian. Thanks also to Andres Martinez and my fellow Schwartz Fellows at the New America Foundation for advice and reactions to the original idea for the book.

Thanks to Rafe Sagalyn and his team for considerably strengthening the book proposal, Tim Bartlett at Basic for sympathetic and helpful shepherding and editing, and Cindy Buck for excellent copyediting.

Notes

CHAPTER ONE

1. Arvind Subramanian, *Eclipse: Living in the Shadow of China's Economic Dominance* (Washington, DC: Peterson Institute, 2011).

2. Gideon Rachman, "Think Again: American Decline: This Time It's for Real," *Foreign Policy* (January–February 2011).

3. Charles Krauthammer, "Decline Is a Choice: The New Liberalism and the End of American Ascendancy," *The Weekly Standard* 15, no. 5 (October 19, 2009).

4. Joseph Nye, "The Decline and Fall of America's Decline and Fall," Project Syndicate, October 6, 2011, available at: http://www.project-syndicate.org/commentary/the-decline-and-fall-of-america-s-decline-and-fall.

CHAPTER TWO

1. Robert Kagan, "Not Fade Away: Against the Myth of American Decline," *The New Republic,* January 17, 2012.

2. Pew Research, Global Attitudes Project, "Global Indicators Database," available at: http://www.pewglobal.org/database/?indicator=17.

3. Thomas L. Friedman and Michael Mandelbaum, *That Used to Be Us: How America Fell Behind in the World It Invented, and How We Can Come Back* (New York: Farrar, Straus & Giroux, 2011).

4. Niall Ferguson, "Why Barack Obama Needs to Go," *Newsweek,* August 19, 2012.

5. Lant Pritchett, "Divergence, Big Time," *Journal of Economic Perspectives* 11, no. 3 (Summer 1997): 3–17.

6. Shaohua Chen and Martin Ravallion, "The Developing World Is Poorer Than We Thought, but No Less Successful in the Fight Against Poverty," *Quarterly Journal of Economics* 125, no. 4 (2010): 1577–1625.

7. The World Bank, World Development Indicators, available at: http://data.worldbank.org/indicator.

8. Ibid.

9. US Department of Commerce, Bureau of Economic Analysis, "Interactive Data: GDP and Personal Income Mapping," available at: http://www.bea.gov/iTable/iTable.cfm?ReqID=99&step=1#reqid=99&step=1&isuri=1.

10. The World Bank, World Development Indicators, available at: http://data.worldbank.org/indicator.

11. Laurence Chandy and Geoffrey Gertz, "Poverty in Numbers: The Changing State of Global Poverty from 2005 to 2015," Global Views Paper (Washington, DC: Brookings Institution, January 26, 2011).

12. Orley C. Ashenfelter, "Comparing Real Wages," Working Paper 18006 (Cambridge, MA: National Bureau of Economic Research, 2012).

13. Michael Clemens, "The Roots of Global Wage Gaps: Evidence from Randomized Processing of US Visas," Working Paper 212 (Washington, DC: Center for Global Development, June 4, 2012).

14. Daron Acemoglu, Simon Johnson, and James A. Robinson, "The Colonial Origins of Comparative Development: An Empirical Investigation," Working Paper 7771 (Cambridge, MA: National Bureau of Economic Research, June 22, 2000).

15. William Easterly, Diego Comin, and Erick Gong, "Was the Wealth of Nations Determined in 1000 BC?" Brookings Global Economy and

Development Working Paper 10 (Washington, DC: Brookings Institution, September 2007).

16. Richard A. Easterlin, "Why Isn't the Whole World Developed?" *Journal of Economic History* 41, no. 1 (1981): 1–19.

17. Ibid., p. 15.

18. UNICEF, "Young Child Survival and Development," available at: http://www.unicef.org/childsurvival/index.html.

19. Fred Pearce, "The Shock of the Old: Welcome to the Elderly Age," *New Scientist,* April 8, 2010.

20. Barro-Lee, "Educational Attainment Dataset," available at: http://www.barrolee.com/.

21. Lant Pritchett, "Where Has All the Education Gone?" *World Bank Economic Review* 15, no. 3 (2001): 367–91.

22. The World Bank, World Development Indicators, available at: http://data.worldbank.org/indicator.

23. George Mason University, "Polity IV Project: Political Regime Characteristics and Transitions, 1800–2012," available at: http://www.systemicpeace.org/polity/polity4.htm.

24. Justin W. van Fleet, Kevin Watkins, and Lauren Greubel, "Africa Learning Barometer" (Washington, DC: Brookings Institution, September 17, 2012), available at: http://www.brookings.edu/research/interactives/africa-learning-barometer.

25. Jishnu Das, Jeffrey Hammer, and Kenneth Leonard, "The Quality of Medical Advice in Low-Income Countries," *Journal of Economic Perspectives* 22, no. 2 (2008): 93–114.

26. Transparency International survey data, available at: http://www.transparency.org/gcb2013.

27. Enrico Spolaore and Romain Wacziarg, "How Deep Are the Roots of Economic Development?" Working Paper 18130 (Cambridge, MA: National Bureau of Economic Research, 2012).

28. William Easterly, Michael Kremer, Lant Pritchett, and Lawrence H. Summers, "Good Policy or Good Luck?" *Journal of Monetary Economics* 32, no. 3 (1993): 459–83.

29. Kenichi Ohmae, *Triad Power: The Coming Shape of Global Competition* (New York: Free Press, 2002).

30. Hongmei Yi, Linxui Zhang, Kim Singer, Scott Rozelle, and Scott Atlas, "Good News, Bad News: Results from a National Representative Panel Survey on China's NCMS," Paper 50104, presented at the 2009 conference of the International Association of Agricultural Economists, Beijing, China, August 16–22, 2009.

31. Eswar Prasad and Raghuram G. Rajan, "China's Key to Sustainable Growth," available at: http://faculty.chicagobooth.edu/raghuram.rajan/research/papers/china%20growth.pdf.

32. Dani Rodrik, "The Future of Economic Convergence," Working Paper 17400 (Cambridge, MA: National Bureau of Economic Research, 2011).

33. International Finance Corporation and The World Bank, "Ease of Doing Business in China," available at: http://www.doingbusiness.org/data/exploreeconomies/china/.

34. Robert W. Fogel, "Why China Is Likely to Achieve Its Growth Objectives," Working Paper 12122 (Cambridge, MA: National Bureau of Economic Research, 2006).

35. Rodrik, "The Future of Economic Convergence," p. 26.

36. Academic Ranking of World Universities, available at: http://www.arwu.org.

37. Fogel, "Why China Is Likely to Achieve Its Growth Objectives."

38. Subramanian, *Eclipse.*

39. Rodrik, "The Future of Economic Convergence."

40. Richard Baldwin, "Trade and Industrialization After Globalization's Second Unbundling: How Building and Joining a Supply Chain Are Different and Why It Matters," Working Paper 17716 (Cambridge, MA: National Bureau of Economic Research, 2011).

41. Ibid., p. 12.

42. United Nations, Department of Economic and Social Affairs, Population Division, "World Population Prospects, the 2012 Revision," available at: http://esa.un.org/unpd/wpp/unpp/panel_population.htm.

43. Subramanian, *Eclipse.*

44. Ibid.

45. Uri Dadush and Bennett Stancil, "The World Order in 2050" (Washington, DC: Carnegie Endowment for International Peace, April 2010).

46. John Hawksworth, "The World in 2050: How Big Will the Major Emerging Market Economies Get and How Can the OECD Compete?" PricewaterhouseCoopers (March 2006), available at: http://www.pwc.com/gx/en/world-2050/pdf/world2050emergingeconomies.pdf.

47. Ibid.

CHAPTER THREE

1. Rachman, "American Decline: This Time It's for Real"; Michael Beckley, "China's Century? Why America's Edge Will Endure," *International Security* 36, no. 3 (Winter 2011–2012): 41–78; Robert A. Pape, "Empire Falls," *National Interest* (January–February 2009); Edward Luttwak, "The Declinists, Wrong Again: The Atlantic Future of the 21st Century," *American Interest* (November–December 2008).

2. YouGov survey administered April 26 to May 2, 2012, results available at: http://www.dartmouth.edu/~benv/files/poll%20responses%20by%20party%20ID.pdf.

3. Subramanian, *Eclipse.*

4. Groningen Growth and Development Centre, Angus Maddison data, available at: http://www.ggdc.net/MADDISON/oriindex.htm.

5. Baldwin, "Trade and Industrialization After Globalization's Second Unbundling."

6. Beckley, "China's Century?"

7. "When Partners Attack," *The Economist,* February 11, 2010.

8. Colum Lynch, "China's Arms Exports Flooding Sub-Saharan Africa," *Washington Post,* August 25, 2012.

9. Kagan, "Not Fade Away: Against the Myth of American Decline."

10. Groningen Growth and Development Centre, Angus Maddison data, available at: http://www.ggdc.net/MADDISON/oriindex.htm.

11. Joseph S. Nye Jr., "The Future of American Power: Dominance and Decline in Perspective," *Foreign Affairs* 89, no. 2 (November–December 2010): 2–12.

12. Carla A. Hills, Dennis Blair, and Frank Sampson Jannuzi, "US-China Relations: An Affirmative Agenda, a Responsible Course," *Council on Foreign Relations* 14 (2007).

13. SIPRI military expenditure data available at: http://portal.sipri.org/publications/.

14. Beckley, "China's Century?"

15. Andrew Nathan and Andrew Scobell, "How China Sees America," *Foreign Affairs* (September–October 2012).

16. See the Ranking America website at: http://rankingamerica.wordpress.com/.

17. David Carey, Bradley Herring, and Patrick Lenain, "Health Care Reform in the United States," Economics Department Working Paper 665 (Paris: OECD, February 2009).

18. OECD, "Figure 1: Comparing Countries' and Economies' Performance," in PISA 2009 database, available at: http://www.oecd.org/dataoecd/54/12/46643496.pdf.

19. The World Bank, World Development Indicators, available at: http://data.worldbank.org/indicator.

20. C. Cindy Fan and Mingjie Sun, "Regional Inequality in China, 1978–2006," *Eurasian Geography and Economics* 49, no. 1 (2008): 1–18.

Chapter Four

1. "Tiger Traps: Asia's Seemingly Relentless Economic Rise Is Still Not Inevitable," *The Economist*, November 17, 2011.

2. Homi Kharas, "The Emerging Middle Class in Developing Countries" (Paris: OECD Development Centre, 2010).

3. Diane Brady, "KFC's Big Game of Chicken," *BusinessWeek*, March 29, 2012.

4. M. Wei, "Starbucks Heads for Smaller China Cities as Coffee Shops Triple," *Bloomberg News*, April 1, 2012.

5. Liesbeth Colen and Johan Swinnen, "Beer Drinking Nations: The Determinants of Global Beer Consumption," LICOS Discussion Paper 270/2010 (Leuve, Belgium: University of Leuven, LICOS Centre for Institutions and Economic Performance, 2010).

6. Daryl Loo, "China's Rx: Foreign-Owned Hospitals," *Business-Week,* June 28, 2012.

7. Tosin Sulaiman, "Africa Attracts Growing Share of Global FDI: Report," *Reuters,* May 3, 2012.

8. Avraham Ebenstein, Ann Harrison, Margaret McMillan, and Shannon Phillips, "Estimating the Impact of Trade and Offshoring on American Workers Using the Current Population Surveys," Working Paper 15107 (Cambridge, MA: National Bureau of Economic Research, 2009).

9. Greg C. Wright, "Revisiting the Employment Impact of Offshoring," Job Market Paper (Davis: University of California, November 2010).

10. Rujuan Liu and Daniel Trefler, "Much Ado About Nothing: American Jobs and the Rise of Service Outsourcing to China and India," Working Paper 14061 (Cambridge, MA: National Bureau of Economic Research, 2008).

11. "FT 500 2012," *Financial Times,* July 19, 2012, available at: http://www.ft.com/intl/companies/ft500.

12. Joel Backaler, "Why the US Needs Chinese Investment," *BusinessWeek,* October 3, 2012.

13. "Tata for Now," *The Economist,* September 10, 2011.

14. OECD iLibrary, "OECD Factbook 2011–2012: Economic, Environmental, and Social Statistics Africa's Trade Partners," available at: http://www.oecd-ilibrary.org/sites/factbook-2011-en/04/01/05/index.html?contentType=&itemId=/content/chapter/factbook-2011-37-en&containerItemId=/content/serial/18147364&accessItemIds=&mimeType=text/html.

15. Christian Broda and John Romalis, "Inequality and Prices: Does China Benefit the Poor in America?" (Chicago: University of Chicago Press, 2008).

16. Christian Broda and David Weinstein, "Are We Underestimating the Gains from Globalization for the United States?" *Current Issues in Economics and Finance* 11, no. 4 (April 2005).

17. David H. Autor, David Dorn, and Gordon H. Hanson, "The China Syndrome: Local Labor Market Effects of Import Competition

in the United States," Working Paper 18054 (Cambridge, MA: National Bureau of Economic Research, 2012).

18. Ebenstein et al., "Estimating the Impact of Trade and Offshoring on American Workers."

19. Federal Reserve Bank of St. Louis, "FRED Economic Data: Graph: All Employees: Manufacturing," available at: http://research.stlouisfed.org/fred2/graph/?chart_texline&s%5b1%5d%5bid%5d =MANEMP&s%5b1%5d%5brange%5d=5yrs; Harold Sirkin, Michael Zinser, and Douglas Hohner, "Made in America, Again: Why Manufacturing Will Return to the US" (Boston: Boston Consulting Group, August 2011), pp. 7–9.

20. Gary C. Hufbauer and Sean Lowry, "US Tire Tariffs: Saving Few Jobs at High Cost," Policy Brief PB12-9 (Washington, DC: Peterson Institute, 2012).

21. Yuqing Xing and Neal Detert, "How the iPhone Widens the United States Trade Deficit with the People's Republic of China," Working Paper 257 (Tokyo: ADBI, 2010).

22. "Hey, Big Spenders," *The Economist*, November 17, 2011.

23. "Unilever Aims to Nearly Double Africa Revenue in Five Years," *Reuters*, May 10, 2012.

24. Knight Frank, "The Wealth Report 2012," available at: http://www.thewealthreport.net/.

25. Tyler Cowen, "What Export-Oriented America Means," *The American Interest* (May–June 2012).

26. IMS Institute for Healthcare Informatics, "The Global Use of Medicines: Outlook Through 2015," May 2011, available at: http://www.imshealth.com/ims/Global/Content/Insights/IMS%20Institute%20for%20Healthcare%20Informatics/Documents/The_Global_Use_of_Medicines_Report.pdf.

27. Kharas, "The Emerging Middle Class in Developing Countries."

28. Stephen Galloway, "Hollywood: How Foreign Audiences Saved Tinseltown," *Foreign Policy* (November 2012).

29. US Department of Commerce, Bureau of Economic Analysis, "US International Trade in Goods and Services" (press release), April

2013, available at: http://www.bea.gov/newsreleases/international/trade
/tradnewsrelease.htm.

30. Shanghai University Academic Ranking of World Universities, available at: http://www.arwu.org/.

31. International Institute of Education (IIE), "Open Doors Report on International Educational Exchange" (New York: IIE, 2011).

32. Adam Ozimek, "The $20 Billion Export Industry That the Government Is Holding Back," *Forbes,* October 9, 2012.

33. KPMG, "Mobilizing Innovation: The Changing Landscape of Disruptive Technologies," available at: http://www.kpmg.com/Global/en/IssuesAndInsights/ArticlesPublications/technology-innovation-survey/Documents/mobilizing-innovation-august-2012.pdf.

34. Subramanian, *Eclipse.*

35. Ping Zhou and Loet Leydesdorff, "The Emergence of China as a Leading Nation in Science," *Research Policy* 35, no. 1 (2006): 83–104.

36. Gert Bruche, "A New Geography of Innovation—China and India Rising," *Columbia FDI Perspectives* 45 (2011).

37. "The World's Most Innovative Companies," *Forbes,* available at: http://www.forbes.com/special-features/innovative-companies.html.

38. "China's Patent Royalty Disconnect," *Financial Times,* May 6, 2013, available at: http://blogs.ft.com/beyond-brics/2013/05/06/chart-of-the-week-chinas-patent-royalty-disconnect.

39. Partnership for a New American Economy, *Patent Pending: How Immigrants Are Reinventing the American Economy* (Washington, DC: Partnership for a New American Economy, 2012).

40. James Lamont, "The Age of 'Indovation' Dawns," *Financial Times,* June 14, 2010.

41. Survey results available from the World Bank at: http://datatopics.worldbank.org/financialinclusion/.

42. Michael Spagat, Andrew Mack, Tara Cooper, and Joakim Kreutz, "Estimating War Deaths an Arena of Contestation," *Journal of Conflict Resolution* 53, no. 6 (2009): 934–50.

43. The World Bank, "Congo, Republic of: Joint Staff Advisory

Note and the Poverty Reduction Strategy Annual Progress Report" (Washington, DC: The World Bank, 2010).

44. UNICEF, "Multiple Indicator Cluster Survey DRC 2010" (New York: UNICEF, 2010).

45. Amanda Glassman, Juan Ignacio Zoloa, and Denizhan Duran, "A Commitment to Vaccination Index: Measuring Government Progress Toward Global Immunization," Policy Paper 9 (Washington, DC: Center for Global Development, August 2012).

46. Victoria Fan, "Europe's Unwelcome Export: Measles," Center for Global Development, December 29, 2011, available at: http://blogs .cgdev.org/globalhealth/2011/12/europe%E2%80%99s-unwelcome -export-measles.php.

47. Yoko Kijima, "Caste and Tribe Inequality: Evidence from India, 1983–1999," *Economic Development and Cultural Change* 54, no. 2 (2006): 369–404.

48. Devesh Kapur, Chandra Bhan Prasad, Lant Pritchett, and D. Shyam Babu, "Rethinking Inequality: Dalits in Uttar Pradesh in the Market Reform Era," *Economic and Political Weekly* 45, no. 35 (2010): 39.

49. Ira N. Gang, Kunal Sen, and Myeong-Su Yun, "Is Caste Destiny? Occupational Diversification Among Dalits in Rural India," Working Paper 162 (Manchester, UK: University of Manchester, Brooks World Poverty Institute, 2012).

50. Kapur et al., "Rethinking Inequality," p. 48.

51. World Values Survey, "Online Data Analysis," available at: http:// www.wvsevsdb.com/wvs/WVSAnalize.jsp.

52. Council on Foreign Relations, "Public Opinion on Global Issues," available at: http://www.cfr.org/thinktank/iigg/pop/.

53. World Values Survey, "Online Data Analysis," available at: http:// www.wvsevsdb.com/wvs/WVSAnalize.jsp.

54. Fareed Zakaria, "The Rise of Illiberal Democracy," *Foreign Affairs* (November–December 1997).

55. Ronald Inglehart and Pippa Norris, "Islamic Culture and De-

mocracy: Testing the 'Clash of Civilizations' Thesis," *Comparative Sociology* 1, nos. 3–4 (2002): 235–64.

56. Christian Davenport and David A. Armstrong, "Democracy and the Violation of Human Rights: A Statistical Analysis from 1976 to 1996," *American Journal of Political Science* 48, no. 3 (2004): 538–54; Christian Davenport, "State Repression and Political Order," *Annual Review of Political Science* 10 (June 2007): 1–23.

57. The World Bank, World Development Indicators, available at: http://data.worldbank.org/indicator.

58. Ibid.

59. George Mason University, "Polity IV Project: Political Regime Characteristics and Transitions, 1800–2012," available at: http://www.systemicpeace.org/polity/polity4.htm.

60. Robert Booth, "WikiLeaks Cables: Jihad? Sorry, I Don't Want to Miss 'Desperate Housewives,'" *The Guardian,* December 7, 2010, available at: http://www.guardian.co.uk/world/2010/dec/07/wikileaks-cables-letterman-housewives-saudi.

61. Zehra F. Arat, "Democracy and Economic Development: Modernization Theory Revisited," *Comparative Politics* 21, no. 1 (1988): 21–36; Robert Jensen and Emily Oster, "The Power of TV: Cable Television and Women's Status in India," Working Paper 13305 (Cambridge, MA: National Bureau of Economic Research, 2007).

62. Inglehart and Norris, "Islamic Culture and Democracy."

63. Dean T. Jamison, Joel G. Breman, Anthony R. Measham, George Alleyne, Mariam Claeson, David B. Evans, Prabhat Jha, Anne Mills, and Philip Musgrove, eds., *Disease Control Priorities in Developing Countries,* 2nd ed. (New York: Oxford University Press, 2006); UN Office on Drugs and Crime, "Intentional Homicide, Count and Rate per 100,000 Population," available at: http://www.unodc.org/documents/data-and-analysis/statistics/Homicide/Homicide_data_series.xls.

64. Bethany Lacina and Nils P. Gleditsch, "Monitoring Trends in Global Combat: A New Dataset of Battle Deaths," *European Journal of Population* 21, no. 2 (2005): 145–66.

65. *The Human Security Report, 2009–2010* (Vancouver BC: Simon Fraser University, 2010).

66. Nathaniel Beck and Richard Tucker, "Democracy and Peace: General Law or Limited Phenomenon?" paper presented at the annual meeting of the Midwest Political Science Association, Chicago (1998); William Easterly, Roberta Gatti, and Sergio Kurlat, "Development, Democracy, and Mass Killings," *Journal of Economic Growth* 11, no. 2 (2006): 129–56.

67. Thomas Friedman, *The Lexus and the Olive Tree* (New York: Farrar, Straus & Giroux, 1999).

68. Solomon W. Polachek and Carlos Seiglie, "Trade, Peace, and Democracy: An Analysis of Dyadic Dispute," in *Handbook of Defense Economics*, vol. 2, ed. Keith Hartley and Todd Sandler (Elsevier, 2007), pp. 1017–73.

69. World Values Survey, "Online Data Analysis," available at: http://www.wvsevsdb.com/wvs/WVSAnalize.jsp.

70. Angus Deaton, "The Financial Crisis and the Well-being of Americans" (2011 OEP Hicks Lecture), *Oxford Economic Papers* 64, no. 1 (2012): 1–26.

CHAPTER FIVE

1. Anthony Leiserowitz, Edward Maibach, Connie Roser-Renouf, and Jay D. Hmielowski, "Climate Change in the American Mind: Public Support for Climate and Energy Policies in March 2012" (New Haven, CT: Yale University and George Mason University, Yale Project on Climate Change Communication, 2012).

2. Paul Cashin and C. John McDermott, "The Long-Run Behavior of Commodity Prices: Small Trends and Big Variability," *IMF Staff Papers* (2002): 175–99.

3. "Crowded Out," *The Economist*, September 24, 2011.

4. Ambrose Evans-Pritchard, "The World's Commodity Supercycle Is Far from Dead," *The Telegraph*, December 2, 2012, available at: http://www.telegraph.co.uk/finance/comment/ambroseevans_pritchard/9717728/The-worlds-commodity-supercycle-is-far-from-dead.html.

5. The speech is available at: http://www.pbs.org/wgbh/american experience/features/primary-resources/carter-energy/.

6. World Energy Council, *Survey of Energy Resources* (London: World Energy Council, 2010).

7. Phillip C. F. Crowson, "Mineral Reserves and Future Minerals Availability," *Mineral Economics* 24, no. 1 (2011): 1–6.

8. US Department of the Interior, US Geological Survey, "Mineral Commodities Summaries 2011," available at: http://minerals.usgs.gov /minerals/pubs/mcs/2011/mcs2011.pdf.

9. US Geological Survey, "Minerals Yearbook, Volume I—Metals and Minerals," available at: http://minerals.usgs.gov/minerals/pubs /commodity/myb/.

10. Emily Sinnott, Augusto de la Torre, and John Nash, *Natural Resources in Latin America and the Caribbean: Beyond Booms and Busts?* (Washington, DC: World Bank Publications, 2010); see also Christa N. Brunnschweiler, "Cursing the Blessings? Natural Resource Abundance, Institutions, and Economic Growth," *World Development* 36, no. 3 (2008): 399–419.

11. Gordon Conway, Jeff Waage, and Sara Delaney, *Science and Innovation for Development* (London: UK Collaborative on Development Sciences, 2010); 2030 Water Resources Group, "Charting Our Water Future: Economic Frameworks to Inform Decision-Making," 2009, available at: http://www.2030waterresourcesgroup.com/water_full /Charting_Our_Water_Future_Final.pdf.

12. European Commission, "European Report on Development 2011–2012" (Brussels: European Commission, 2011); Conway et al., *Science and Innovation for Development.*

13. Jonathan A. Foley, Navin Ramankutty, Kate A. Brauman, Emily S. Cassidy, James S. Gerber, Matt Johnston, and David P. M. Zaks, "Solutions for a Cultivated Planet," *Nature* 478, no. 7389 (October 20, 2011): 337–42.

14. Conway et al., *Science and Innovation for Development.*

15. Foley et al., "Solutions for a Cultivated Planet."

16. Conway et al., *Science and Innovation for Development.*

17. 2030 Water Resources Group, "Charting Our Water Future."

18. Vaclav Smil, "Water News: Bad, Good, and Virtual," *American Scientist* 96 (2008): 399–407.

19. Amartya Sen, *Poverty and Famines: An Essay on Entitlement and Deprivation* (Oxford: Oxford University Press, 1983), p. 175.

20. Idean Salehyan, "From Climate Change to Conflict? No Consensus Yet," *Journal of Peace Research* 45, no. 3 (2008): 315–26.

21. Richard Black, "Climate Summit Set for Rows on Flying, Cash, and History," *BBC News*, November 5, 2011.

22. For references, see The World Bank, "Exploring Climate and Development Links," available at: http://climate4development.worldbank .org/.

23. Nicholas H. Stern, *Stern Review: The Economics of Climate Change*, vol. 30 (London: HM Treasury, 2006).

24. Nebojsa Nakicenovic, Joseph M. Alcamo, Gerald R. Davis, Bert de Vries, Jørgen Fenhann, Stuart R. Gaffin, and Zhou Dadi, *Special Report on Emissions Scenarios: A Special Report of Working Group III of the Intergovernmental Panel on Climate Change*, PNNL-SA-39650 (Richland, WA: Pacific Northwest National Laboratory, Environmental Molecular Sciences Laboratory, 2000). Agriculture data from The World Bank, World Development Indicators, available at: http://data .worldbank.org/indicator.

25. Emmanuel Skoufias, Mariano Rabassa, and Sergio Olivieri, "The Poverty Impacts of Climate Change: A Review of the Evidence," World Bank Policy Research Working Paper Series 5622 (Washington, DC: The World Bank, 2011).

26. World Health Organization (WHO), "Global Health Risks: Mortality and Burden of Disease Attributable to Selected Major Risks" (Geneva: WHO, 2009).

27. Peter W. Gething, David L. Smith, Anand P. Patil, Andrew J. Tatem, Robert W. Snow, and Simon I. Hay, "Climate Change and the Global Malaria Recession," *Nature* 465, no. 7296 (2010): 342–45.

28. Douglas Gollin and Christian Zimmermann, "Global Climate

Change, the Economy, and the Resurgence of Tropical Disease," *Mathematical Population Studies* 19, no. 1 (2012): 51–62.

29. Matthew E. Kahn, "The Death Toll from Natural Disasters: The Role of Income, Geography, and Institutions," *Review of Economics and Statistics* 87, no. 2 (2005): 271–84.

30. Juliette Jowit and Patrick Wintour, "Cost of Tackling Global Climate Change Has Doubled, Warns Stern," *The Guardian,* June 25, 2008.

31. Roger Pielke Jr., "Climate of Failure," *Foreign Policy,* August 6, 2012.

32. The World Bank, World Development Indicators, available at: http://data.worldbank.org/indicator.

33. Qi Ye, "China's Low-Carbon Development," Brookings Institution, May 31, 2011, available at: http://www.brookings.edu/events/2011/05/31-china-carbon.

34. David Wheeler, "Fair Shares: Crediting Poor Countries for Carbon Mitigation," Working Paper 259 (Washington, DC: Center for Global Development, 2011); James Kanter, "A 'Big Thumbs Up' for Renewable Energy," *New York Times*, June 3, 2011.

35. Morgan Bazilian, Ijeoma Onyeji, Michael Liebreich, Ian MacGill, Jennifer Chase, Jigar Shah, Dolf Gielen, and Shi Zhengrong, "Re-considering the Economics of Photovoltaic Power," *Renewable Energy* 53 (May 2013): 329–38.

36. Aaron Wiener, "Made in the Shade," *Foreign Policy,* July 9, 2012; Jake Schmidt and Aaron Haifly, "Delivering on Renewable Energy Around the World: How Do Key Countries Stack Up?" Natural Resources Defense Council, available at: http://www.nrdc.org/energy/files/delivering-renewable-energy.pdf.

CHAPTER SIX

1. Ipsos Public Affairs, "Ipsos Poll Conducted for Reuters, August 2012," available at: http://www.ipsos-na.com/download/pr.aspx?id=11840.

2. Martin Johnson and Chris Rasmussen, "Jobs Supported by Exports: An Update" (Washington, DC: US Department of Commerce, 2012).

3. Congressional Budget Office, "Estimated Impact of the American Recovery and Reinvestment Act on Employment and Economic Output from April 2012 Through June 2012" (Washington, DC: CBO, 2012).

4. Subramanian, *Eclipse;* Vincent Trivett, "The TRUTH About Who Really Owns All of America's Debt," *Business Insider,* July 20, 2011, available at: http://www.businessinsider.com/who-owns-us -debt-2011-7.

5. Frederic Docquier and Hillel Rapoport, "Globalization, Brain Drain, and Development," *Journal of Economic Literature* 50, no. 3 (2012): 681–730.

6. Caglar Ozden, Christopher R. Parsons, Maurice Schiff, and Terrie L. Walmsley, "Where on Earth Is Everybody? The Evolution of Global Bilateral Migration, 1960–2000,"*World Bank Economic Review* 25, no. 1 (2011): 12–56; US Census Bureau, "Current Population Survey—March 2010 Detailed Tables," available at: http://www.census .gov/population/foreign/data/cps2010.html.

7. Carl Lin, "Give Me Your Wired and Your Highly Skilled: Measuring the Impact of Immigration Policy on Employers and Shareholders," IZA Discussion Paper 5754 (Bonn: Institute for the Study of Labor, 2011).

8. Vivek Wadhwa, AnnaLee Saxenian, Ben Rissing, and Gary Gereffi, "America's New Immigrant Entrepreneurs: Part I," Science, Technology, and Innovation Paper 23 (Durham, NC, and Berkeley: Duke University School of Engineering and University of California School of Information, 2007); John Gibson and David McKenzie, "Eight Questions About Brain Drain," *Journal of Economic Perspectives* 25, no. 3 (2011): 107–28.

9. Murat Genc, Masood Gheasi, Peter Nijkamp, and Jacques Poot, "The Impact of Immigration on International Trade: A Meta-Analysis," IZA Discussion Paper 6145 (November 2011).

10. Gabriel J. Felbermayr and Benjamin Jung, "The Pro-Trade Effect of the Brain Drain: Sorting Out Confounding Factors," *Economics Letters* 104, no. 2 (2009): 72–75; Maurice Kugler and Hillel Rapoport, "Migration, FDI, and the Margins of Trade," CID Working Paper 222 (Cambridge, MA: Harvard University, Center for International Development, June 2011).

11. Patricia Cortes and Jessica Pan, "The Relative Quality of Foreign Nurses in the United States," CReAM Paper 1231 (London: University College London, Department of Economics, Centre for Research and Analysis of Migration, June 2012).

12. Gianmarco I. Ottaviano and Giovanni Peri, "Rethinking the Effects of Immigration on Wages," Working Paper 12497 (Cambridge, MA: National Bureau of Economic Research, 2006); Gianmarco I. Ottaviano, Giovanni Peri, and Greg C. Wright, "Immigration, Offshoring, and American Jobs," Working Paper 16439 (Cambridge, MA: National Bureau of Economic Research, 2010).

13. Jeffrey Passel and D'Vera Cohn, "US Unauthorized Immigration Flows Are Down Sharply Since Mid-Decade" (Washington, DC: Pew Hispanic Center, 2010); Eric Smalley, "These May Be the Droids Farmers Are Looking For," *Wired*, November 11, 2011; Tom Baxter, "How Georgia's Anti-Immigration Law Could Hurt the State's (and the Nation's) Economy" (Washington, DC: Center for American Progress, 2011).

14. Alan Barrett and Bertrand Maître, "Immigrant Welfare Receipt Across Europe," IZA Discussion Paper 5515 (Bonn: Institute for the Study of Labor, 2011).

15. Lesley Williams Reid, Harald E. Weiss, Robert M. Adelman, and Charles Jaret, "The Immigration-Crime Relationship: Evidence Across US Metropolitan Areas," *Social Science Research* 34, no. 4 (2005): 757–80; Alpaslan Akay, Amelie F. Constant, and Corrado Giulietti, "The Impact of Immigration on the Well-being of Natives," IZA Discussion Paper 6630 (Bonn: Institute for the Study of Labor, 2012).

16. United Nations, Department of Economic and Social Affairs, Population Division, *World Population to 2300* (2004), available at: http://www.un.org/esa/population/publications/longrange2/World Pop2300final.pdf; Jeffrey S. Passel and D'Vera Cohn, "US Population Projections, 2005–2050" (Washington, DC: Pew Research Center, 2008).

17. Moshe Hazan and Hosny Zoabi, "Do Highly Educated Women Choose Smaller Families?" Discussion Paper 8590 (London: Centre for

Economic Policy Research, 2011); Grayson K. Vincent and Victoria A. Velkoff, "The Next Four Decades: The Older Population in the United States: 2010 to 2050" (Washington, DC: US Department of Commerce, Economics and Statistics Administration, US Census Bureau, 2010).

18. The World Bank, World Development Indicators, available at: http://data.worldbank.org/indicator.

19. D. A. Shields, "Previewing Dairy Policy Options for the Next Farm Bill" (Washington, DC: Congressional Research Service, 2010).

20. Welfare Information, "Payments," available at: http://www.WelfareInfo.org/payments/.

21. Judd Legum, "Rep. King Designs Electrified Fence for Southern Border: 'We Do This with Livestock All the Time,'" ThinkProgress, July 13, 2006, available at: http://thinkprogress.org/politics/2006/07/13/6259/king-fence/.

22. Charles Kurzman, "Why Is It So Hard to Find a Suicide Bomber These Days?" *Foreign Policy* (September–October 2011).

23. Michael Gerson and Alison Lawler Russell, "American Grand Strategy and Seapower" (conference report), CNA Analysis & Solutions, November 2011, available at: http://politicalscience.osu.edu/faculty/jmueller/CNApart.pdf; Michael Cooper, "Happy Motoring: Traffic Deaths at 61-Year Low," *New York Times,* April 1, 2011.

24. "TSA Top 10 Good Catches of 2011," The TSA Blog, January 5, 2012, available at: http://blog.tsa.gov/2012/01/tsa-top-10-good-catches-of-2011.html.

25. Bruce Schneier, "The TSA Proves Its Own Irrelevance," Schneier on Security, January 9, 2012, available at: http://www.schneier.com/blog/archives/2012/01/the_tsa_proves.html.

26. Josh Boak, "US Looks to Foreign Tourism to Add Jobs, Revenue," *Politico,* March 27, 2012, available at: http://www.politico.com/news/stories/0312/74552.html.

27. Shan Carter and Amanda Cox, "One 9/11 Tally: $3.3 Trillion," *New York Times,* September 8, 2011.

28. John Mueller and Mark Stewart, "Terror Security and Money," paper presented at the annual convention of the Midwest Political Science Association, Chicago, April 1, 2011.

29. Doris Meissner, Donald M. Kerwin, Muzaffar Chishti, and Claire Bergeron, "Immigration Enforcement in the United States: The Rise of a Formidable Machinery" (Washington, DC: Migration Policy Institute, 2013), available at: http://www.migrationpolicy.org/pubs /enforcementpillars.pdf.

30. Beckley, "China's Century?" p. 49.

31. Brad de Long said this on his blog, available at: http://delong .typepad.com/sdj/2006/04/morning_coffee_8.html.

32. YouGov survey administered April 26 to May 2, 2012, results available at: http://www.dartmouth.edu/~benv/files/poll%20responses %20by%20party%20ID.pdf.

33. Dan Gardner, "The Decade of Horror That Wasn't," *Ottawa Citizen*, September 7, 2011.

34. German Marshall Fund, *Transatlantic Trends: Immigration Survey* (Washington, DC: German Marshall Fund, 2011).

CHAPTER SEVEN

1. National Geographic, "National Geographic–Roper Public Affairs 2006 Geographic Literacy Study," available at: http://www.national geographic.com/roper2006/pdf/FINALReport2006GeogLitsurvey.pdf.

2. Raisa Belyavina and Rajika Bhandari, *US Students in Overseas Degree Programs: Key Destinations and Fields of Study* (Institute for International Education, 2012).

3. Ibid.

4. David Smith, "Portuguese Escape Austerity and Find a New El Dorado in Angola," *The Guardian*, September 15, 2012; Alasdair Fotheringham, "Europe's Jobless Flee for New El Dorados," *The Independent*, March 18, 2012.

5. British Council, *Broadening Horizons: Breaking Through the Barriers to Overseas Travel* (London: British Council, 2013).

6. College Board, "Big Future: College Costs: FAQs," available at: https://bigfuture.collegeboard.org/pay-for-college/college-costs /college-costs-faqs; Pew Research, *Is College Worth It? College Presidents, Public Assess Value, Quality, and Mission of Higher Education* (Washington, DC: Pew Research, May 16, 2011).

7. The rankings used for the subsequent discussion were taken from Academic Ranking of World Universities, "Academic Ranking of World Universities—2010," available at: http://www.arwu.org/ARWU2010.jsp; The World University Rankings (*Times Higher Education*), "World University Rankings 2011–2012," available at: http://www.timeshigher education.co.uk/world-university-rankings/2011-2012/top-400.html; and TopUniversities, available at: http://www.topuniversities.com/.

8. OECD, "Foreign/International Students Enrolled," OECD .StatExtracts, available at: http://stats.oecd.org/Index.aspx?Dataset Code=RFOREIGN.

9. Devex.com, "Candidate Sourcing," available at: http://www .devex.com/en/candidate-sourcing; http://siteresources.worldbank.org /EXTHRJOBS/Resources/1058432-1304013341703/faq.html.

10. African Economic Outlook, available at: http://www.african economicoutlook.org/en/.

11. Jenny C. Aker and Isaac M. Mbiti, "Mobile Phones and Economic Development in Africa," Working Paper 211 (Washington, DC: Center for Global Development, 2010).

12. V. Curtis and S. Cairncross, "Effect of Washing Hands with Soap on Diarrhoea Risk in the Community: A Systematic Review," *The Lancet: Infectious Diseases* 3, no. 5 (2003): 275–81.

13. Knight Frank, "The Wealth Report 2012," available at: http:// www.thewealthreport.net/.

14. Health Care Cost Institute, "2010 Health Care Cost and Utilization Report," available at: http://www.healthcostinstitute.org/2010 report.

15. Bumrungrad International Hospital, http://www.bumrungrad .com/thailandhospital.

16. Aaditya Mattoo and Randeep Rathindran, "Does Health Insur-

ance Impede Trade in Health Care Services?" Policy Research Working Paper 3667 (Washington, DC: The World Bank, 2005).

CHAPTER EIGHT

1. The World Bank, World Development Indicators, available at: http://data.worldbank.org/indicator.

2. Thomas Bollyky, "Forging a New Trade Policy on Tobacco," Policy Innovation Memorandum 7 (Washington, DC: Council on Foreign Relations, 2011).

3. Shirley Jahad, "Homeland Security Cracks Down on Cyber Piracy," KPCC Public Radio, June 30, 2010, available at: http://www.scpr.org/news/2010/06/30/16776/homeland-security-and-ice-crack-down-cyber-piracy/.

4. Arvind Subramanian, "Medicines, Patents, and TRIPS," *Finance and Development* (March 2004): 22–25.

5. David Kravets, "Hollywood-Funded Study Concludes Piracy Fosters Terrorism," *Wired*, March 3, 2009; Motion Picture Association of America, "Report on Trade Barriers to Exports of US Filmed Entertainment" (Washington, DC: MPAA, 2009).

6. Ruth Towse, Christian Handke, and Paul Stepan, "The Economics of Copyright Law," *Review of Economic Research on Copyright Issues* 5, no. 1 (2008): 1–22.

7. Tobias Schonwetter, Jeremy de Beer, Dick Kawooya, and Achal Prabhala, "Copyright and Education: Lessons on African Copyright and Access to Knowledge," *African Journal of Information and Communication* 10 (2009–2010): 37–52.

8. Autor, Dorn, and Hanson, "The China Syndrome."

9. Wolfgang Dauth, Sebastian Findeisen, and Jens Suedekum, "The Rise of the East and the Far East: German Labor Markets and Trade Integration," IZA Working Paper 6685 (Bonn: Institute for the Study of Labor, 2012).

10. U.S. House of Representatives, Permanent Select Committee on Intelligence, "Investigative Report on the US National Security Issues Posed by Chinese Telecommunications Companies Huawei and

ZTE," October 8, 2012, available at: http://intelligence.house.gov/sites /intelligence.house.gov/files/documents/Huawei-ZTE%20Investigative %20Report%20(FINAL).pdf.

11. World Intellectual Property Organization (WIPO), "International Patent Filings Set New Record in 2011," March 5, 2012, available at: http://www.wipo.int/pressroom/en/articles/2012/article_0001.html #annex2.

12. Data from International Air Transport Association (IATA), http://www.iata.org/.

13. Neli Esipova, Julie Ray, and Rajesh Srinivasan, "Gallup World Poll: Young, Less Educated Yearn to Migrate to the US," April 30, 2010, available at: http://www.gallup.com/poll/127604/young-less-educated -yearn-migrate.aspx; Neli Esipova, Julie Ray, and Anita Pugliese, "Gallup World Poll: The Many Faces of Global Migration," International Organization for Migration (IOM) Migration Research Series 43 (2011), available at: http://publications.iom.int/bookstore/free/MRS43.pdf.

14. US Department of State, Bureau of Consular Affairs, "Diversity Visa Program (DV-2011)—Selected Entrants," available at: http://travel .state.gov/visa/immigrants/types/types_5073.html.

15. Karin Fischer, "Foreign Enrollment in US Graduate Schools Remains Flat, Survey Finds," *Chronicle of Higher Education,* November 10, 2009; Organization for Economic Cooperation and Development, *Education at a Glance 2011* (Paris: OECD, 2011).

16. Vivek Wadhwa, *The Immigrant Exodus: Why America Is Losing the Global Race to Capture Entrepreneurial Talent* (Philadelphia: Wharton Digital Press, 2012).

17. Jeffrey Passel, D'Vera Cohn, and Ana Gonzalez-Barrera, "Net Migration from Mexico Falls to Zero—and Perhaps Less" (Washington, DC: Pew Hispanic Center, April 23, 2012).

18. NHS Employers, "List of Developing Countries," April 16, 2013, available at: http://www.nhsemployers.org/RecruitmentAnd Retention/InternationalRecruitment/Code-of-Practice/Pages/developing -countries.aspx.

19. Gibson and McKenzie, "Eight Questions About Brain Drain"; United Nations Conference on Trade and Development, *Impact of Remittances on Poverty in Developing Countries* (Geneva: UNCTAD, 2011).

20. Docquier and Rapoport, "Globalization, Brain Drain, and Development"; Michael Clemens, "Do Visas Kill? Health Effects of African Health Professional Emigration," Working Paper 114 (Washington, DC: Center for Global Development, 2007).

21. Antonio Spilimbergo, "Democracy and Foreign Education," Working Paper 5934 (Washington, DC: International Monetary Fund, 2007).

22. William Easterly and Ariell Reshef, "African Export Successes," Working Paper 16597 (Cambridge, MA: National Bureau of Economic Research, December 2010).

23. Chris McComb, "About One in Four Americans Can Hold a Conversation in Another Language," Gallup News Service, April 6, 2001, available at: http://www.gallup.com/poll/1825/about-one-four-americans-can-hold-conversation-second-language.aspx.

24. Nancy C. Rhodes and Ingrid Pufahl, "Foreign Language Teaching in US Schools: Results of a National Survey" (Washington, DC: Center for Applied Linguistics, 2010).

25. US Department of State, Bureau of Educational and Cultural Affairs, "The Fulbright Program," available at: http://fulbright.state.gov/uploads/ce/34/cc34fcd6b62b90e41d83d2b77ba1040d/2008-2009-Fulbright-Annual-Report.pdf.

26. Deloitte Center for Health Solutions, "Medical Tourism: Consumers in Search of Value" (2008), available at: http://www.deloitte.com/assets/Dcom-unitedStates/Local%20Assets/Documents/us_chs_MedicalTourismStudy(3).pdf.

CHAPTER NINE

1. Chicago Council on Global Affairs, "Chicago Council Surveys: Foreign Policy in the New Millennium" (surveys released September

10, 2012), available at: http://www.thechicagocouncil.org/files/Surveys/2012/files/Studies_Publications/POS/Survey2012/2012.aspx.

2. "World Carbon Dioxide Emissions Data by Country: China Speeds Ahead of the Rest," posted by Simon Rogers and Lisa Evans on Datablog: Facts Are Sacred, *The Guardian,* January 31, 2011, available at: http://www.guardian.co.uk/news/datablog/2011/jan/31/world-carbon-dioxide-emissions-country-data-co2#data.

3. Duncan Clark, "Phasing Out Fossil Fuel Subsidies 'Could Provide Half of Global Carbon Target,'" *The Guardian,* January 19, 2012.

4. OECD, "Inventory of Estimated Budgetary Support and Tax Expenditures for Fossil Fuels," available at: http://www.oecd.org/site/tadffss/48805150.pdf.

5. John Baffes and Tassos Haniotis, "Placing the 2006/08 Commodity Price Boom into Perspective," Policy Research Working Paper Series 5371 (Washington, DC: The World Bank, 2010).

6. Todd Moss and Ben Leo, "IDA at 65: Heading Toward Retirement or a Fragile Lease on Life?" Working Paper 246 (Washington, DC: Center for Global Development, 2011).

7. OECD, "OECD Data Lab," available at: http://www.oecd.org/statistics/.

8. G. Demombynes and S. Trommlerova, "What Has Driven the Decline of Infant Mortality in Kenya?" Policy Research Working Paper 6057 (Washington, DC: The World Bank, 2012); UNICEF, "UN Commission Sets Out Plan to Make Life-Saving Health Supplies More Accessible" (press release), September 26, 2012, available at: http://www.unicef.org/media/media_65942.html.

9. John Norris and Connie Viellette, "Five Steps to Make Our Aid More Effective and Save More Than $2 Billion," *USAID Monitor* (Washington, DC: Center for Global Development, 2011).

10. Sen, *Poverty and Famines.*

11. William Easterly, "What Did Structural Adjustment Adjust? The Association of Policies and Growth with Repeated IMF and World Bank Adjustment Loans," *Journal of Development Economics* 76, no. 1 (2005): 1–22.

12. Joseph Hanlon, Armando Barrientos, and David Hulme, *Just Give Money to the Poor: The Development Revolution from the Global South* (Sterling, VA: Kumarian Press, 2010).

13. Chandy and Gertz, "Poverty in Numbers."

CHAPTER TEN

1. Jesse M. Shapiro, "Smart Cities: Quality of Life, Productivity, and the Growth Effects of Human Capital," Working Paper 11615 (Cambridge, MA: National Bureau of Economic Research, 2005).

2. Ed Glaeser, Jed Kolko, and Albert Saiz, "Consumer City," Working Paper 7790 (Cambridge, MA: National Bureau of Economic Research, 2000).

3. Edward Harris and Frank Sammartino, "Trends in the Distribution of Household Income Between 1979 and 2007," in *Measuring Economic Sustainability and Progress,* ed. Dale W. Jorgenson, J. Steven Landefeld, and Paul Schreyer (Cambridge, MA: National Bureau of Economic Research, 2012).

4. William Easterly, "The Middle-Class Consensus and Economic Development," *Journal of Economic Growth* 6, no. 4 (2001): 317–35.

5. Samuel Bowles and Herbert Gintis, "The Inheritance of Inequality," *Journal of Economic Perspectives* 16, no. 3 (2002): 3–30.

6. Miles Corak, *Chasing the Same Dream, Climbing Different Ladders: Economic Mobility in the United States and Canada* (Economic Mobility Project, PEW Charitable Trusts, 2010), available at: http://www.pewtrusts.org/news_room_detail.aspx?id=56877.

7. Thomas Piketty and Emmanuel Saez, "The Evolution of Top Incomes: A Historical and International Perspective," Working Paper 11955 (Cambridge, MA: National Bureau of Economic Research, 2006).

8. Anthony B. Atkinson, Thomas Piketty, and Emmanuel Saez, "Top Incomes in the Long Run of History," Working Paper 15408 (Cambridge, MA: National Bureau of Economic Research, 2009).

9. Isabel Ortiz and Matthew Cummins, "Global Inequality: Beyond the Bottom Billion: A Rapid Review of Income Distribution in

141 Countries," *Child Poverty and Inequality in New Perspectives,* Social and Economic Policy Working Paper (New York: UNICEF, 2011).

10. Miles Corak, "Do Poor Children Become Poor Adults? Lessons from a Cross-Country Comparison of Generational Earnings Mobility," *Research on Economic Inequality* 13 (2006): 143–88.

CONCLUSION

1. "Leading Through Civilian Power: The First Quadrennial Diplomacy and Development Review" (Washington, DC: US Agency for International Development, 2010), available at: http://www.state.gov/documents/organization/153108.pdf.

2. The White House, "National Security Strategy" (Washington, DC: The White House, May 2010), available at: http://www.white house.gov/sites/default/files/rss_viewer/national_security_strategy.pdf.

Index